The Quantur

"The Quantum Akashic Field is open for exploration to all who develop a systematic strategy of meditation and creative imagination. By sharing his own out-of-body experiences, recorded through the years in his personal journals, Jim Willis serves as our guide into that world of mystery and revelation."
— **GEORGE NOORY**, host of *Coast to Coast AM*

"Jim Willis, through a combination of modern science and very personal experience, manages to produce a veritable DIY guide for anyone interested in out-of-body experience (OBE). This book should cause the steadfast nonbeliever to admit that there is at least a scientifically based possibility that the OBE phenomenon is plausible and provides validation as well as explanations and encouragement for those who have experience with OBEs. If ever there was a successful explanation for the inexplicable, this book is it."
— **GERRY BAILEY**, computer scientist, systems engineer, and OBE practitioner

"Willis weaves together science, metaphysics, and cultural references in a thoughtful exploration of the out-of-body experience. Using his fascinating and highly symbolic personal experiences, he gently but logically guides us to see that OBEs are a natural part of our spiritual development. This book is a great summary of the basics, with inspiring personal examples, encouragement, and practical guidance that is both useful for the beginner and a valuable refresher for those looking to enhance their experience.
— **WILLIAM BUHLMAN**, author of *Adventures Beyond the Body*

"Another brilliant book by Jim Willis. How he manages to make complex concepts so easily accessible, I don't know. Read it at your own risk!"
— **ELYN AVIVA**, PhD, MDiv, author of *The Question: A Magical Fable*

"Combining cutting-edge theories, mysticism, and personal narratives, Jim Willis provides a fascinating overview of the out-of-body experience. Willis seamlessly makes connections between such diverse topics as perception, consciousness, philosophy, shamanism, and quantum physics, which challenges readers to look beyond their present assumptions about who and what they really are."
— **PAUL J. LESLIE**, psychotherapist, author, educator, author of *The Art of Creating a Magical Session*

"This is a very dangerous book. With his ability to tell a good story, Jim Willis can draw you right out of your body and into the astral planes. So, if you choose to read it, don't say you haven't been warned."

— GARY WHITE, PhD, professor emeritus at Iowa State University
and coauthor of the Powerful Places guidebook series

"Accessing the fabled Akashic records has always been a curiosity of mine, and in his book *The Quantum Akashic Field* Jim provides a fun and easy-to-understand guide for exploring this sacred domain."

— CLIFF DUNNING, host and producer of *Earth Ancients* podcast

"Jim Willis has written a wonder-filled, magical book. Thoroughly acquainted with the theoretical principles of the new physics and how they relate to the problem of consciousness, he offers sage practical advice on how to achieve a conscious out-of-body experience and navigate the challenging terrain of non-ordinary states of consciousness.... Marinated in the narrow, intellectualistic rationalism of our mainstream Western culture and an equally narrow and dogmatic fundamentalist form of Christianity, Willis shares how he managed to free himself from these mental prisons and experience ever-wider, more expansive and inclusive states of awareness."

— JOSEPH M. FELSER, Ph.D., professor of philosophy at
Kingsborough Community College, author of *The Way Back to Paradise* and
The Myth of the Great Ending, and former board member of the Monroe Institute

The Quantum Akashic Field

A Guide to Out-of-Body
Experiences for the
Astral Traveler

Jim Willis

FINDHORN PRESS

Findhorn Press
One Park Street
Rochester, Vermont 05767
www.findhornpress.com

Text stock is SFI certified

Findhorn Press is a division of Inner Traditions International

Disclaimer
The information in this book is given in good faith and intended for information only.
Neither author nor publisher can be held liable by any person for any loss or damage
whatsoever which may arise from the use of this book or any of the information therein.

Cataloging-in-Publication data for this title is available from the Library of Congress

ISBN 978-1-62055-953-6 (print)
ISBN 978-1-62055-954-3 (ebook)

Printed and bound in the United States by Lake Book Manufacturing, Inc.
The text stock is SFI certified. The Sustainable Forestry Initiative® program
promotes sustainable forest management.

10 9 8 7 6 5 4 3 2 1

Edited by Michael Hawkins
Text design and layout by Anna-Kristina Larsson
This book was typeset in Cormorant and Raleway

To send correspondence to the author of this book, mail a first-class letter to
the author c/o Inner Traditions • Bear & Company, One Park Street, Rochester,
VT 05767, USA and we will forward the communication, or contact the author
directly at **www.jimwillis.net**

For Sobuko
My forever friend and guide

Contents

PART TWO
THE PRACTICE

Introduction

"The Master Game involves the quest for spiritual awakening, enlightenment, and liberation. The goal is to discover one's own true nature and to know from direct, empirical experience that this nature is both sacred and immortal."
Hank Wesselman in *Visionseeker*

What If?

What if someone were to tell you that your five senses of touch, sight, smell, hearing, and taste, important senses that have evolved to help you relate to and interact with the world around you, also serve as filters that cut you off from a true experience of the totality of reality? What if that person were to further explain that the scientific method, that marvelous, systematic, investigative technique that relentlessly explores, tracks down, measures, and describes the world around us, is insufficient to fully explain the nature of the cosmic ocean in which we live and move and have our very being? And what if you were to learn that almost everything you have been taught about reality is an illusion?

Would you accept it? Would you believe it? Would it change your life?

Most people would probably respond with an emphatic, "No! I'm doing just fine, thank you!"

But the fact that you chose to even begin reading this book proves you are probably not like most people.

You are curious. You sense that there is something going on beneath the surface of your day-to-day life. You have read enough to know that new discoveries in almost every scientific discipline are overturning the safe and comfortable story of existence that has been the staple of academic life for generations. You have watched enough of the History Channel on TV to begin to suspect that most religions, as practiced today, don't truly represent the teachings of their original founders. You have become aware that ancient texts, these days readily available via the Internet, offer puzzling enigmas and mysterious allusions which suggest that our distant ancestors seemed to be in touch with forces we have long forgotten—forces that may have atrophied due to disuse but still lie dormant deep within, waiting for us to access them.

In this book we're going to explore some of these ideas. Together, we will seek avenues that lead to a reality outside the normal perception realm of most contemporary experience. We'll discover that what many of us have been taught is insufficient. We'll try to penetrate to the essence of the freedom that lies just beyond our waking consciousness. Call it quantum perception.

When we, either by accident or intentional design, somehow bypass our senses while still fully awake and aware, we discover that consciousness is not a by-product of our brains. It doesn't originate in the brain at all. It is universal. The brain is an *organizer*, not a *producer*, of consciousness. It is more like a radio than a generator. Once we bypass the filters of our five senses and connect to universal consciousness outside our familiar sensory parameters, the effect can be staggering. We realize we are more than our bodies—that our bodies simply house our essence.

It's as simple, and as complicated, as that. Out-of-Body and Near-Death Experiences occur when we are able to do an end run around our highly evolved sensory filters. When we escape the prison of our senses we achieve freedom. All that is becomes accessible. We have penetrated the quantum realm.

Let me share an entry from a dream journal that I've kept on and off for years:

September 4, 2012

I'm fully alert, even though my body is relaxed. I try to remain calm and patient so as to let things unfold at their own rate. An image pops into my mind, totally unbidden. It's a picture of a monkey, hopping up to a window in his cage. I notice that the window is open. There's nothing to stop the monkey from jumping outside. I immediately interpret that as meaningful. I am the monkey and I can leave my cage—my body.

Then the scene changes. I see a gate—iron bars standing between stone pillars. But the gate is open. I can walk through if I want. After some mental struggle I stand at the open gate and gaze out onto a magnificent vista. Way below me is a whole universe of towns and villages. I ask to change into a hawk so I can fly over the whole thing and see it from above. When that doesn't happen I ask to fall into it—toward it. I await some spectacular result.

But then it occurs to me that even this, as magnificent as it is, is a mental construct of my own. So I ask to see Reality, not my own idea of reality.

Suddenly the whole image rolls up like a scroll. For just a second I stare into a huge nothingness. I experience it as music—walking into music. For one, brief moment, I am aware of a tremendous pulsing throughout the core of my body. My heart and chest are pulsing—there is no other word that quite describes it. It's not uncomfortable at all. If anything, it's just the opposite. The feeling is wonderful. I feel it, and am conscious that I am feeling it, and it feels profoundly peaceful. I really don't want it to end, but I realize that my journey for today is almost over. I went a little farther than ever before, and have the feeling that's the way it's going to be. Each day, one more step. Gradually. Inch by inch.

Unseen worlds glimpsed in dreams and visions comprise the very realms, spruced up with newly minted scientific vocabulary, that shamans, dowsers, and mystics have been exploring for thousands of years. And it's closer than you can imagine!

Our Objective

Our objective is simply stated, if not quite so simply achieved:

When you finish this book, I hope you will have *both* the desire to perceive dimensions that are now filtered out by your five senses *and* a good idea of how to go about achieving that desire.

That's the goal. Someday, when your body ceases to function, you will experience those dimensions. Everyone does, because everyone dies. But why not at least view some coming attractions so you will know what to expect and be better prepared when the time comes? Why not experience reality now?

I well remember a phone call I received late one night. A good friend of mine was dying and wasn't expected to live until morning. This man had led an exemplary life throughout. He had founded a college, enjoyed a successful teaching career, served in various local political offices, and made a small fortune along the way. He was also a deacon in the church and had the reputation of being a well-respected pillar of the community. His nurse said he had asked for me, his minister, so of course I got out of bed and quickly made my way to be with him.

I found him in tears. When I asked if he was ready to cross over he said something I will never forget: "Jim, for my whole life I have done everything but the one thing that was most important. I never prepared for this moment."

We were lucky. He made it through that long night and lasted for ten more. I spent a few hours of every one of those next few days with him. I hope I was able to help. I don't know if I taught him anything. I know he taught me a lot.

This book, hopefully, will help you be better prepared than my friend, the college professor.

The Method We Will Follow

In Part One we're going to study the theory behind Out-of-Body Experiences. We'll look at the difference between dreams and visions and explore ways in which imagination can serve a much greater purpose than mere fantasy. We'll learn about maintaining fully conscious perception without relying on the filtering effects of the five senses.

What kind of help from the other side can we expect? Do spirit guides, our "Higher Self," or guardian angels exist? How do we interpret what appears to be a bizarre, totally unfamiliar landscape? This section will serve as an OBE (Out-of-Body Experience) primer.

Then, after a brief excursion into the history, anecdotal evidence and science undergirding OBE research, we'll move on to Part Two. There we'll begin to discover techniques which will help us have the experience ourselves. We don't need to learn exotic methods or experiment with illegal hallucinogens. There are safe, time-tested and simple meditative techniques which, if practiced diligently, can aid us in moving out of body within the safe confines of our own homes. Perceiving reality outside the prison of our senses is possible for everyone. This section of the book will give us a focused place to start.

Werner Heisenberg, the Nobel Prize-winning physicist, once said, "The first gulp from the glass of natural sciences will turn you into an atheist, but at the bottom of the glass God is waiting for you."

My response?

Drink up, everyone! The Quantum Akashic Field awaits! Let's begin.

PART ONE
THE THEORY

THEORY INTRODUCTION

"Man's ordinary state of consciousness, his so-called waking state,
is not the highest level of consciousness of which he is capable.
In fact, this state is so far from real awakening that it could
appropriately be called a form of waking sleep."
Robert De Ropp in *The Master Game*

The "Real World" Illusion

Seeing beyond the illusion of what we call the "real" world is not easy. It hasn't been for more than a hundred years, a century that featured solid scientific research. It takes work and discipline.

Pinch yourself, for instance, and your body seems solid. Your senses insist this is the case. It seems to be an essential, irrevocable truth. But the plain facts of science, regardless of what normally seems so patently obvious, prove that your senses are deceiving you. You are not solid. You are a churning, seething, bundle of energy. Subatomic particles within your body and your surroundings are zooming in and out of material existence, some surviving for only a matter of seconds or less before disappearing and being replaced. Cells are forming, reproducing and sloughing off your skin. Internal organs are performing their functions without your knowledge or overt consent. Despite your feelings of permanence, you are on a journey that eventually leads to old age and death. That's called life, and there is simply no denying it.

But wait! There's more! The entity that you call "you" is a mass of perpetual motion, no matter how peaceful and still you may feel. You inhabit a galaxy that is hurtling through space, while standing on a planet that is orbiting the sun and revolving on its axis at the same time. What this means is that if you are an average reader, in the time it took you to read this paragraph, given the fact that you are rushing along through space at 530 miles (853 kilometers) per second, you are now more than 8,000 miles (12,875 kilometers) away from the point you were when you began reading.

Given that reality, maybe it's time to rethink the whole idea of what it *is* and what it *means* to be alive and conscious. If we can't trust a point of view that seems to be centered within us, maybe it's time to visualize a new perspective—one that better conforms to these physical facts we know to be true.

The whole conception of a non-material "you," whether we call it consciousness, soul, essence, or ego, that resides in a body or brain, is obsolete. It's not wrong. It's simply insufficient.

We refer to this essence when we say "my brain" or "my body" or "my foot." Where does the one who says "my" reside? What part of the body houses your "my?" Is there an essential organ or structure that is indispensable to the "I" who says "my?"

We used to say it was the heart. When the heart stopped beating, life ceased. Then we learned how to keep people alive with artificial hearts.

We once said it lived in the brain. But then we learned how to keep people alive even after they were pronounced "brain-dead."

More and more it becomes obvious that our essence, the essential entity we call "I," resides only temporarily in our material bodies. From time to time it seems as though it escapes its confines. That's what Out-of-Body and Near-Death Experiences are. Our immaterial essence seems to move away from our material bodies while fully conscious. We gain a new perspective. We change, quite literally, our point of view.

Perceiving reality from outside your material body is not a mystical, "woo-woo" experience. It is extraordinarily common. It has a long and illustrious history going back thousands upon thousands of years, and forms the basis of virtually every religion on earth. The experience is backed up by reputable scientific data, has been studied and reported in medical journals, and is still an object of protocol in virtually every major hospital whenever a patient regains consciousness after undergoing clinical death.

Even our language betrays its presence:

"My life passed before my eyes!"

"I thought I'd died and gone to heaven!"

"If I should die before I wake I pray the Lord my soul to take."

So if we're going to take OBEs seriously the first hurdle we face is to *examine* them seriously. That's not easy in a world prone to sarcasm and ridicule of anything outside normal experience.

When my book, *Supernatural Gods,* came out I was interviewed on many radio shows and podcasts. Most of the interviews were fun and informative. The hosts were open and receptive. One, however, revealed a typically close-minded attitude that is all too common these days.

"Why do you insist that meditation is so important?" the host exclaimed. "I don't meditate and I'm doing just fine!"

All I could do was shake my head. Here was a man who didn't meditate, which was fine, I suppose. It seemed to be working for him. But despite his lack of knowledge he felt qualified to criticize something about which he, by his own admission, had no familiarity.

That's a difficult obstacle to overcome in polite conversation.

If you are new to the Out-of-Body Experience, if you are either trying to understand something that happened to you in a dream or waking vision, or searching for your own initial waking OBE, rest assured that there is good science behind the whole subject. You don't have to check your intellect at the door. You don't have to be religious or spiritual. Indeed, sometimes such things even get in the way.

OBEs, by their very nature, *feel* mystical and supernatural. After all, although they occur outside the arena of the senses we still have to use our sense-governed intellect to interpret and describe them when they're over. That can make them sound other worldly. But they don't require appealing to gods or angels. There are no higher powers you have to appease. You don't have to atone for your sins or ask to be blessed by a "consecrated" authority.

Instead, they are rooted in simple, scientifically-based principles that underlie the very nature of biological life itself. Physicists have only quite recently discovered a whole quantum-based reality that mystics, shamans, and dowsers have been exploring for thousands of years. But since that discovery, practical researchers and mystic practitioners of what has sometimes been called the metaphysical arts are now traveling the same highway. One group found their way into the fast lane by using complex mathematics. The other arrived through the use of intensive intuitive skills. But each contributed a language and road map that describe a similar experience.

A Brief History

Early in the twentieth century Albert Einstein demonstrated to a handful of physicists that time and space, the very cornerstones of what we experience as the "real" world, are not fixed, stable entities. Up until then everyone assumed that the one thing we could count on, aside from death and taxes, was that a minute was always a minute and a mile always a mile. "Minute" and "mile," or kilometer, were words we used to identify how much time had passed and how far we had traveled. They may be earth-bound measurements, but anyone, anywhere in the galaxy or the universe, who agreed to use those arbitrary measurements, could understand exactly how much time had passed or exactly how far something had traveled.

Then along came Einstein, who taught us that both distance and duration were relative to the local situation of the observer.

It gets worse. In 1919 a scientist by the name of Ernest Rutherford split an atom. Ever since the time of the Greeks, atoms had been thought to be the building blocks of everything. There was nothing smaller than an atom. But when Rutherford split an electron off from an oxygen atom he proved that what had previously been considered to be the building block of all nature was, in fact, made up of smaller particles.

Where was this going to end? Was nothing sacred?

As it turns out—no.

Werner Heisenberg soon developed his uncertainty principle. He answered the question "What is light?" with a multiple choice. It was either a wave or a particle, depending on how you chose to measure it. What an idea! A scientist could now determine the properties of light, depending on how he decided to look at it. He could choose! And his choice determined the outcome as much as anything inherent in light itself.

Paul Dirac, Erwin Schrödinger, and others went on to prove again and again to those who were curious enough to follow their theories, that how we perceive the universe is, in fact, an illusion.

There were many educated people who heard these theories, scoffed at them, and said, "I know what I see! I know what I experience! These guys are just pie-in-the-sky talkers who have no practical sense at all!" According to everyday principles, the scoffers were exactly right. If you drop a brick on your foot, it hurts. No amount of lecturing by a physicist, who tells you the brick and your foot are only perceived realities, is going to take away the pain. A tangible aspirin works much better.

But on another level, a strictly scientific one, Einstein, Heisenberg, Dirac, and Schrödinger were right. And they were only the tip of the iceberg. In 1916, Bertrand Russell and Alfred North Whitehead had set out to prove that mathematical systems were purely logical. They couldn't do it. Instead Kurt Gödel, in 1931, proved that no system of mathematics could be proven by its own, or any other, set of rules. Even Russell's colleague at Cambridge, Ludwig Wittgenstein, seemed to conspire against him. Wittgenstein insisted that language itself was not to be trusted. He believed that "logical" descriptions of "real" situations were misguided at best, and possibly even outright deceptions. Together, all these folks concluded that we cannot simply look at the world, describe what we see, and arrive at conclusions as to what it really is. Everything is subjective. Everything is relative. It all depends on context—who we are, where we are, and what we see.

In short, given the state of modern science and the traditions of religious thought we have inherited, it now appears certain that there is more to life than that which we perceive with our senses. There are unseen worlds that influence our perception of reality. What's more, they actually form it! And although we cannot observe those worlds with the microscopes and telescopes now available, we can explore them when we learn to bypass our five senses and move out and away from the body they define and regulate.

There are still many people who will read these words and say, "I know what I see!" No one will ever convince them that they have bought into the illusion. Such is its power over us. How strange it is that truth itself appears as a magical mirage.

But for thousands of years there have been those who saw through the illusion even though they had no way of quantifying their insights. By examining their dreams and visions, through carefully controlled and disciplined intuitive exercises, and by following the experiential threads of mystic inward journeys, they arrived at the conclusion that there are other worlds out there, awaiting exploration.

These worlds can appear downright strange at times when we try to describe them using language that was invented to explain things with which we are all familiar. After all, they are totally outside our experience. We can't come back from such a journey and say, "This is what I saw!" The best we can say is, "What I saw looked something like this!"

Take this example from my journal, for instance. The experience happened many years ago but still seems as vivid as the day I wrote about it:

November 2, 2012

I wake up just before 3:30 and, with a lot of mental reservations, decide to meditate. (It's cold outside the covers!) I go into the living room, sit in the chair I use for meditation, and turn on some soft music…

I affirm to myself that I am more than my body. I try to keep all external thoughts at bay. That doesn't work, of course, so I mentally step outside myself and become the Watcher, who simply observes the person who is doing all this frantic thinking. With that simple step, everything changes. I see my body lying in the chair as a separate entity, a vehicle for consciousness. But I am outside. What does the Watcher look like? I don't have the slightest idea. I can describe my body in the chair. But that's all.

What happens next is very difficult to describe…

I am covered with a piece of something that looks like cardboard. Maybe I'm in a box. But the cardboard is easily removed, perhaps with some help from someone else. I'm not certain. Then confusion. I ask for clarity. Then I take off.

Soaring—flying free—twisting and turning—tumbling—freedom—joy.

At one point I seem to approach a defining horizon. Above is light. Pure light. Not even light, really, just blazing whiteness. Below is darkness. But the darkness is dotted with pinpricks of light. It seems to be the universe. For a moment, an immense being, I think it's me, holds the darkness in his hand. He is smiling. I feel that he could enter that universe at any time and at any place, with just a thought. Then he holds, not the universe, but an old fashioned cigar box. This, too, contains something, but I don't know what it might be. Perhaps it is the universe. Perhaps just my body. But he kneels as he studies it intently.

Next I see pillars of light either supporting or being drawn towards the light. One of them is rooted at some earthly vortex. Another seems to come from the Medicine Wheel I recently built in a valley below our house. There are many more. They form some kind of structure that reaches towards the world of light. It's as if they form great pillars that support the sky— Stonehenge on steroids or Disney gone berserk. But maybe they simply connect the two worlds. I don't know.

How can an image so incredibly visual and real be so hard to describe with words?

By now an hour has gone by and the CD music starts over for the third time. I am conscious of the fact that I can stay out longer if I wish. But somehow I am too full of images and pictures. It's time to return. So I do.

Meanings

I have no idea what happened during that hour of meditation. I don't know if it contained some sort of message or not. It felt as though it did, but if so, the message eludes me to this day, many years later. I am fully aware that it might have been a kind of lucid dream, a freedom-wish fantasy from my subconscious. After all, I'd been wrapped up in the usual worldly cycle of tasks that consume us all. Good things. Practical things. But I often feel that such a mind-set cuts us off from Spirit. There are reasons mystics go out in the deserts or up on mountain tops to get away from humdrum necessities. As important as these daily tasks seem, and they are important, they are trivial compared with the real work of Reality. After all, if I am that Being who's "got the whole world in his hands," the choice of what color to paint the kitchen cabinets is really not very important.

So whether it was a lucid dream, fantasy, or OBE, that makes at least the basic message easy to decipher.

"I am more than my body!"

Amen to that!

Moving Forward

The task now before us is to examine the theory behind Out-of-Body Experiences. What's the difference between dreams, visions and fully fledged OBEs? Can we chalk it all up to imagination? Is there any empirical data that suggests we can actually "move" outside our bodies while fully conscious? If so, what actually "moves?" If it *is* possible to move outside material reality, what will we perceive? Are the ancient stories and myths about spirit guides or helpers who live in unseen realms really true? Do such beings exist? And what else can we expect to find "out there?" These are the questions to which we now turn.

ONE
DREAMS AND VISIONS

*"**Dream:** A series of thoughts, images, or emotions occurring during sleep.*
__Lucid Dream:__ A dream in which the sleeper is aware that he or she is dreaming
and is sometimes able to control or influence the course of the dream.
__Vision:__ Something seen in a dream, trance, or ecstasy; especially a supernatural
appearance that conveys a revelation."
Merriam-Webster Dictionary

The World of Dreams

Where does imagination stop and reality begin? How can you tell the difference between something that happens in your experience and something that happens in your mind, given the fact that anything that happens "outside" has to be eventually interpreted by our brains, which are most definitely "inside?"

These are tough questions. Joseph Campbell, the college professor who, more than anyone else, brought the study of mythology into public consciousness after his conversations with Bill Moyers were broadcast on the PBS special, *The Power of Myth*, once said that dreams are a great source of the spirit. There are cultures that take dreams much more seriously than contemporary western audiences. The Aborigines of Australia regularly "dream the fire" and consider what they call the Dream World to be more real than the outward world of illusion we call normal life. The traditional closing words each evening spoken by the innkeepers who were called the "Keepers of the Shrine" in Celtic folklore, were always the same: "May the Gods send you a dream."

But what are dreams?

The truth is, no one really knows.

There are lots of ideas, of course.

Henry David Thoreau once called dreams the "touchstones of our characters."

Robert Moss, in his book, *Dreamgates*, wrote:

"Our physical reality is surrounded and permeated by the vigorous, thrumming life of the realms of spirit and imagination to which we return, night after night, in dream. There is no distance between the Otherworld and its inhabitants and our familiar, sensory reality; there is only a difference in frequency."

In this age of amazing and awe-inspiring scientific revelations about how the body works, in this age of discoveries concerning mitochondrial DNA and cell reproduction, in this age of Technicolor NASA flights and Mars Rovers, an amazing fact stands out above all else. At least it seems amazing to me. We have been sleeping and dreaming for millions of years, and no one knows why.

That's right. No one. In spite of comprehensive research coming out of thousands of sleep clinics established coast to coast and around the world, the first and greatest commandment of sleep research is this: *No one knows why we sleep.* And the second is like unto it: *No one knows why we dream, either.*

Sigmund Freud was the first modern psychiatrist to bring the study of dreams to the attention of the general public. His theory of dreams was that they were a representation of unconscious desires, motivations, and thoughts. He came to believe that we are driven by sexual and aggressive instincts that, due to social pressures, we repress from our conscious awareness. Because these thoughts are not consciously acknowledged, they find their way into our awareness through dreams. In his book, *The Interpretation of Dreams*, Freud wrote that dreams are "disguised fulfillments of repressed wishes."

J. Allan Hobson and Robert McCarley suggested that dreams are a symbolic interpretation of signals generated by the brain during sleep. The symbols, if interpreted correctly by a trained analyst, can reveal clues which help us understand what is going on in our subjective unconscious.

A more contemporary idea emerged as computers caught on. When your home computer "sleeps" at night—in other words, when you're not using it—some programs automatically kick in. They spend time cleaning up and organizing "clutter," defragmenting and systematizing things so the computer will work more efficiently. This dream model speculates that your brain operates in the same way. When you "shut down" in sleep, your brain goes to work organizing all the thoughts and external stimuli you encountered during the day.

Yet another theory proposes that dreams operate as a kind of therapeutic psychotherapy session. Your brain tries to make sense out of things while you sleep in the safe environment of your bed, somewhat akin to a therapist's couch. Things that happen to you are analyzed for meaning and projected on the wall of your conscious mind when you wake up and remember. Your emotions help make sense of the symbols.

We might very well discover that one or more of these models is correct. Perhaps the truth lies in combining parts of all of them. But for thousands of years shamans and mystics have taught that in dreams our normal waking consciousness is let out to play. It separates from its confines within the material body and brain and returns to its mystic union with the One. That is the purpose of sleep, they remind us. Without this daily renewal, life in the material world would simply be too hard to endure.

Modern sleep-deprivation and dream-deprivation studies seem to indicate that this is, indeed, the case. When we are tired and deprived of sleep, our creativity goes first. Then we start to forget things. Finally we go completely mad and die. In this day and age we may not fully understand what sleep and dreaming are all about, but we know that the material body ceases to function without them. Death is the result. That seems a pretty good indication that the ancients knew something about the importance of dreaming.

What this means is that dreams might well be considered another name for Out-of-Body Experiences, without which we would soon go mad and die.

Traditional shamans go even further. They claim that when released from the normal bounds of restraints of the waking, analytical hemisphere in our brains, our true nature, our consciousness, returns to the Source. They believe that with practice we can actually follow along while fully conscious. In dreams we perceive parallel dimensions in which we learn truths that guide our waking activities. The trick is to intentionally apply those truths to our waking experience.

Consider this example, for instance, from my own dream journal:

July 24, 2012

I own property and am with a surveyor who is laying out a line that will add acreage to what I already own. In the dream, the surveyor ran the line and I saw that it encompassed a lot of land. There was a pond, woods, and a lovely mountain that adjoined my land. It was a paradise and I almost couldn't believe what I was about to acquire.

But when I tried to walk down the new line I got lost. I kept veering, somehow, to the right. I was venturing into territory where other people lived. It became more and more crowded and uncomfortable. Knowing the newly surveyed line demarcating my acquisition was over to the left, I finally found a sort of unpleasant woman and her son who would guide me back to my land. But when the woman guided me to the left and toward my property, she led me into a walk-in safe, much as you would find in a bank. I had the impression that we were underground, but still somehow on the way to my new land. She said to me, "This is where we (meaning she and her son) have to live when you die." She began closing the door behind her, and, spinning the combination lock, opened another door that made up one of the walls. Behind that there was another door . . . and another . . . and another. I began to have a claustrophobic attack.

"How do I get out of here?" I asked, with some real concern. I noticed colored lines, black and red, painted on the door and corresponding wall.

"It's easy," she said. "Just remember, black on black and red on red." I had the impression that the colored lines had to match up in order to open the door.

Then, just as a moment of real claustrophobia struck, I woke up, sweating and breathing hard, as if I was experiencing a panic attack.

A Possible Interpretation

At that time of my life I was newly retired from active Christian ministry. It was only natural that I viewed the dream through my still-familiar Christian perspective. (If religious terminology doesn't work for you here, substitute vocabulary from your own spiritual or metaphysical perspective.) In doing so it led me into a new way of thinking that was more in line with a fresh spirituality that was just beginning to percolate down into my psyche. It seemed to me back then that the new land I was surveying represented new spiritual dimensions that were opening up to me, adding to my spiritual "acreage," as it were. It was beautiful, and promised to add much to my inner experience. In short, it represented the new things I was learning about reality and spiritual truth. It was shown to me by the surveyor, a guide, who obviously knew what he was doing. This was a representation of a spiritual helper.

But when I tried to negotiate this land on my own I got lost. It was unfamiliar ground. It began to feel to me that I was straying back into my old life—crowded and uncomfortable. The "woman," I have come to believe, represented my ego. The "safe" was either my body or the left hemisphere of my brain, the place where our egos live. When we die and return to inconceivable beauty and unity in the One, our ego will die. So it wants us to stay here, in the "safe" of our bodies, because when we are finished with this body and make the journey home, our ego, our sense of separateness, dies. *"This is where we have to live when you die,"* the old woman had said. In that sense, the "safe" was really a grave.

I suppose this concept is at the root of what Christian theology calls demon possession. Read allegorically, we *are* demon possessed. The "demon" is our ego, who is threatened whenever we move toward wholeness. Is this "demon" a spiritual entity? You bet it is! But it is a demon of our own making. It is the ego, "fallen" from grace, the grace of Wholeness and Unity, "cast out" of paradise in order to live a life of separateness. The "Christ," that part of us who exists in paradise on the other side but remains with us here as well, the one who has "become flesh" yet "dwells in us"—the one who is "perfect man and perfect God" in hypostatic union—the "Light"—the one who watches over us—grants us power to "cast out demons in his name."

In other words, again using Christian terminology, recognizing our "Christ nature" gives us the power to exercise dominion over our lifelong battle with separation and loneliness even though we are constantly, and have always been, in perfect unity with all that is.

So how do we "drive out" or escape from the demon? *"It's easy,"* she said. *"Just remember, black on black and red on red."*

This phrase stumped me for two days. Then I found a possible answer in a book by Ted Andrews. It's called *Animal Speak: The Spiritual & Magical Powers of Creatures Great and Small.* While talking about totemic animals he mentions that Owl and Hawk are often found in tandem. One is a creature of the night, the other of the day. One's color in nature is black, as in night. The other's is red, as in "red-tailed hawk." Black is the color of the feminine in nature. It represents earth and dark places such as caves and caverns. Red is masculine. Male birds often display red feathers and features during courting rituals. Red flowers attract humming birds and bees for pollination. Red draws attention to itself. It has often been my color, the color of the cardinal, the bird named after the hierarchy of the church. I always seem to have a favorite red shirt hanging in my closet. Significantly, it is also the color of blood—the blood of sacrifice. Although it may be pushing things, red and black were the colors of my first High School. (Okay—maybe that's going too far, even for me!)

Black and red. Night and day. Yin and Yang. Feminine and Masculine. Consider this experience I had one memorable afternoon shortly after I had my dream:

I decided one day to take my trombone down to our Medicine Wheel and play some music just to see what might happen. Our dog, Rocky, always ready for adventure, tagged along. When I got to the gig, feeling quite foolish if the truth were known, I didn't have the foggiest idea where to begin. I just decided to wing it, so I began to play a few bars of a George Gershwin song, *Someone to Watch Over Me*. Rocky is a tough audience. He immediately sat down and began to howl along with me. Then, even though it was 3:00 in the bright afternoon, about four owls, from all directions, began to hoot back at me. I picked up their song and began to imitate it musically. My jazz background kicked in. I would play their notes and then riff on them a little and they would answer back. We had quite a session going until I got tired and had to quit. I think they probably would have gone on all afternoon. But the commotion promptly caught the attention of a high-flying hawk, who added a shrill "Kreeee" to the performance. That shut everybody up.

Why were owls hooting in the middle of the afternoon? They are creatures of the night. And why, out of all the thousands of songs in my head, did I start to play *Someone to Watch Over Me*? Did I subconsciously select a song that revealed that I was searching for something? And where does hawk fit in?

Now let's put it all together. Owl and hawk represent female and male and, more important in this case, those sides of the brain which are often called feminine and masculine, but are more accurately labeled intuitive and analytical. In other words, right and left hemisphere.

How do you get "out" of the body that will be the decaying home of ego when we die? *"It's easy," the woman said. "Just remember, black on black and red on red."* It takes both hemispheres of our brain, working together. Intuition is valuable. But so is analysis. Feeling is important. But so is understanding.

The World of Visions

In many Indian tribes, a Native American youth was not considered an adult unless he had experienced a vision. After a solitary period of preparation he would seek guidance from a spirit helper, usually an animal envoy. Upon receiving his vision he would carry with him, for the rest of his life, a symbol of this new totem animal. It might be a feather or bit of fur, depending on the animal that had appeared to him. He would place it carefully in a medicine bag or pouch and it would never leave his side.

I'm rational and of scientific bent, not given to ecstatic experiences. But I am also an incurable romantic. For forty years I was a Protestant clergyman who lived most of his waking hours in the left side of his brain, meaning I am normally self-contained to a fault. Often, for me, religion was a matter of "knowing about" rather than "experiencing."

But for almost five decades I was also a professional musician. I started playing in dance bands in 1960. I loved to watch people dance, but I couldn't dance myself. It's not that I didn't have rhythm or couldn't learn simple moves. It's just that every time I tried to walk onto a dance floor a palpable, almost physical, force would say, "Stop!" It bothered me for years. I even talked to a psychologist friend about it once, thinking that if I could learn to dance I could open up secret doors in my psyche that I didn't even know were there.

His advice? "Loosen up!"

Didn't work.

As the twentieth century drew to a close I spent time one summer at a cabin I had built in the woods of western New England, communing with nature while getting in touch with some issues that were on my mind. Five feet in front of the cabin's porch was a rock, about four feet long, lying on its side. Obviously forces other than those found in nature had been employed to work the top smooth, and I had often wondered why it appeared to be almost face-like.

I spent afternoons for four days in this setting, meditating on whatever came to mind, trying to go deeper into myself than I normally do. By the second day I was conscious of sounds that I first thought were caused by cars on the highway, about a mile away. It was not until the fourth afternoon that I realized I was hearing the sounds in my right ear, which is completely deaf.

After a moment, it came to me that what I was hearing was not highway noise, but drums. Suddenly I was aware that I had snapped my eyes wide open and was experiencing a fully formed sentence ringing in my head. Even though my heart was racing, I didn't hear a voice and I saw no apparition. I hadn't been thinking about dancing at all, but the sentence that seemed to appear, almost floating before my eyes, was, "It's not that you can't dance. It's that you won't dance."

As soon as I saw, heard, or somehow experienced that message I felt, rather than figured out, that the reason I could not dance was because, at one time, dance was so sacred, either to me or the people who danced on this spot of ground, that I could not sully it by reducing it to mere entertainment.

I am probably one of the most rational people you will ever meet. For most of my life I wasn't sure if I believed in reincarnation or not, and I only believed in spirits on the occasional second Tuesday. But in that instant, I looked down at the rock I had been contemplating for the last four days and somehow *knew* that it was meant to be standing upright.

Fearing that, any minute, I would discover a perfectly acceptable psychological explanation for what was happening to me, I immediately got a shovel and began excavating around the rock. It took about an hour to dig down to bedrock, only about a foot deep on this ledge, clearing a six-foot circle surrounding the stone. I knew long before I finished what I was going to find.

Hidden beneath the soil at the base of the rock was a tripod of stones, obviously placed by human hands. They were formed to exactly fit the bottom of the rock. And in a semicircle, spread fan-shaped to the east, were seven hammer stones that could only have been made by pre-Columbian people.

The next day, when I used a hydraulic jack and ropes to stand the stone on its pedestal, the smoothed face of the stone swung just a fraction around toward the southeast, facing exactly the place where I had earlier determined that the sun peeked over a faraway ridge on the morning of the spring equinox.

In doing research about the indigenous people of my area, I later discovered a possible explanation for the rock. It stands on a natural divide. All the water from the stream to its east eventually flows into a huge reservoir to the south. The water draining from the swamp to the west flows out to the Connecticut River and the Atlantic Ocean at Long Island Sound. This would have made the area a natural place of power to the people who lived here. But the rock itself stood on a small plateau, a natural stage. On all four sides a tribe could have gathered to watch a religious ritual "in the round," so to speak. Was this toppled rock a centerpiece of that ritual?

One explanation for the stone being knocked over might lie in unsubstantiated stories about religious disagreements between Indians and Europeans in early New England. When Indians watched Puritans burying their dead, they thought they both worshiped a common deity. The Puritans used four-foot-high rocks as headstones for graves. Some Indian tribes had similar rituals. They danced around the rock as they prayed for the departed. But Puritans were taught that while their rocks were sacred, Indian rocks were heathen idols. So the Puritans knocked them down whenever they came across them.

I had compiled a list with the names of every person who had owned that property since 1798 when the town was first settled. It is easy to believe that the very first pioneer who farmed this land, which was awarded to his ancestral family as pay for participation in King Philip's War, came across this spot in his sheep pasture and, recognizing it for the pagan idol it was, knocked it down, to the glory of God.

There it lay until I, his future town minister, put it back up, also to the glory of God.

I was so impressed by the whole affair that I told some folks about it. One thing led to another and we wound up having a dedication service there on the night of the winter solstice. Not knowing what to do, we drank some mead and burned some incense, hoping the spirit of the place would accept our good intentions.

And that was that until March. On a day of early thaw I walked out to the place for the first time since December. The snow had melted back from around the base of the rock, just as it had around many other rocks in the area. But at the foot of this special rock lay the feathers, not the carcass, just the feathers, of a ruffed grouse.

My first thought was that a hawk had killed a grouse on this spot. Nine days out of ten, I still believe that. But I called my daughter that day to tell her the story. She knows a lot about all things Indian and I mentioned the grouse. She called me back a few minutes later and I could hear the excitement in her voice.

"Dad, I looked up the meaning of having the ruffed grouse as your totem animal." She then read to me, "When the Creator sends you the grouse as your spirit guide, it is a message to attune yourself to the dance of life. Its keynote is sacred dancing and drumming, both powerful ways in their own right to invoke energies ... rhythmic movement is a part of life ... all human activity is a kind of dance and ritual."

What do I make of all this? I don't have the faintest idea. My rational self accepts the coincidence of a hawk killing a grouse at this particular time and place. But why a *grouse*, especially given its ancient meaning relating to my own dance phobia? Why this particular time? Why *this* rock, out of all the many others? And why does it tie in to my discovering the secret of the rock after my time of meditation, exactly when I was attempting to let the woods sort out my confused mindset? And why just *feathers*, with no carcass?

I don't really know, but I once told this tale to an Ojibwa teaching Elder after an all-day seminar. We had spent the day sitting in a circle, learning about his tribe's creation myths. Much to my dismay, while I related my experience he appeared rather bored.

As I told the story and commented on his seeming lack of interest, he said, "Okay, the grouse was on the west side of the rock. What next?"

"I didn't tell you it was on the western side of the rock. How did you know that?"

"Because that's where we would have expected it to be. That's the direction the soul takes its leave when it departs. Honestly, why do you Christian preachers always expect your God to answer prayer, but act surprised when ours does?"

Dumbfounded, I asked, "Do you mean to tell me I've been searching for an experience with God all my life and now I discover He's an Indian?"

"No," he said grinning back with a cherubic expression. "*She's* an Indian!"

I don't carry a medicine bag, but I had one of the grouse feathers laminated in plastic. I carry it in my wallet. And some more feathers are mounted in a picture frame on my back porch. Along with the feathers are these words from Ted Andrews:

> "Grouse ... of the Sacred Spiral,
> Leading us on,
> To reach the everlasting heights,
> Where we can live as one."

Now comes the next-to-final chapter of this vision quest. A few years ago, with our new house built and the scars of construction fading quickly from the recovering landscape, I meditated one afternoon and felt my Consciousness easily slip from my body. For once I was able to simply be rather than try to force a "happening." One of the biggest traps while practicing meditation is to try to repeat a past experience. So I simply surrendered to whatever would happen and went with the flow of the spirit.

I found myself moving out the door and standing in our gazebo, overlooking the Medicine Wheel. I stood with my arms raised, as though in prayer. Then I was at the Medicine Wheel itself, still standing with my arms raised to the Cosmos. Across the central stone stood an ancestor. Was she a spirit guide? I simply don't know for sure. But I asked the ancestor to dance with me and held out my hands. We whirled around the circle for a while, but something told me this wasn't how you did it. So I asked her to teach me. Step by step, heel and toe, I learned what seemed to be an ancient dance. It was as if I was transported back to a time when tribes of ancestral Americans danced around a fire, perhaps on this very spot of ground.

But then things began to change. The only way I can try to describe it is that I began to grow on the inside. The Medicine Wheel was inside me, and then the whole property on which we were dancing, and then the whole world, and then the whole universe. It was all inside me. I contained the whole material universe. (Words here are simply insufficient.) Somehow I could see the dance of time, of the Cosmos itself, expressing itself in movement.

To be honest, I didn't want it to end. But eventually I opened my eyes and found myself back in familiar surroundings. I went to tell my wife, Barb, about it, still feeling expanded and free. Then, remembering my very first vision beside the first standing stone way up in New England, a thousand miles away, she spoke aloud the words that had hung suspended before my eyes on that day long ago. Until that moment, I had forgotten them:

"It's not that you can't dance. It's that you won't dance."

And now I was dancing! I had come full circle. The words remembered from many years ago, the prophecy of my vision, had come true:

When the Creator sends you the grouse as your spirit guide, it is a message to attune yourself to the dance of life. Its keynote is sacred dancing and drumming, both powerful ways in their own right to invoke energies ... rhythmic movement is a part of life ... all human activity is a kind of dance and ritual.

Had I finally begun to dance to the music of the spheres? Had the rhythms of earth energy begun to work their way into the very fiber of my being—the same rhythms our ancestors heard so many thousands of years ago?

I'll never know, of course. At least I'll never be able to prove it to a skeptic's satisfaction. All I know is that I've had dreams while sleeping, and visions while fully awake. They are different, to be sure. But both seem exceptionally powerful and vivid.

Could such things really be possible? Can we sometimes glimpse through the veil to see snapshots of hidden realities?

It's always possible, of course, to pull the wool over our own eyes. Sometimes we simply believe what we want to believe. But coincidence goes only so far. It seems to me that sometimes we employ the word to give us an excuse not to believe what our senses tell us is foreign to our normal experience. It's a comfort to be able to say, "Oh, it's just coincidence."

But it doesn't take much of a shift to consider plain facts that, as unbelievable as they might seem, might be pointing toward unseen realities.

Dreams and Visions: The Connection

There's more to this story. Here's the final chapter. We've been examining dreams and visions. Obviously they exhibit differences. One happens when we're sleeping, the other while we're awake. But once in a while they overlap.

Let me share a final dream/vision. When it occurred I was fully awake and sitting in a chair in our gazebo, which overlooks the Medicine Wheel down in the valley below. At the same time, I must confess that I was meditating pretty deeply. I had no thoughts of trying to imagine anything or make up a story.

Indeed, I was engaged in something quite different. I was trying to eliminate all thoughts. I was attempting to achieve perfect peace. Then, quite unexpectedly, a full-blown story appeared in my mind as if it were a movie on screen. It seemed as though I was watching a drama unfold. This is what I saw. You be the judge:

August 12, 2012: An early morning meditation

She always enjoyed that time of the year when her family traveled to this hilltop to gather the stone blanks they needed to make tools for the coming year. Folks would come from far away each spring. It was a time of celebration and companionship—a time for sharing food and the closeness of the fire circle. The old people told stories and the young caught up with news from all over. It was a time for weddings and dancing.

For many years now she had felt a kinship with the stones they found here. They were bright and beautiful—good material for working into tools, but also somewhat mystical. It was as if the stones contained a hidden magic, a message they would reveal if only you held them long enough and listened carefully.

Once she had found, right here on this hill, a small rock that, with only a few well-placed strokes of her small hammer stone, she shaped into the image of a hawk, a bird she especially respected. Hawk was her spirit messenger. She kept the hawk/stone with her at all times while they visited this quarry, and then hid it carefully in a special place above the shore line where she could easily find it when they returned during the next season.

But this year was a time of rains and storm. On the eve of the day they had decided to leave they experienced the biggest storm yet. Water rose to the place where they often played and fished. She felt compelled to go and see that her hiding place for hawk was safe.

No one saw what happened next. They only knew that she disappeared during the flood. Had the bank collapsed? Had she stood too close to the edge? Her family called and called, searching in the storm for any sign of her, but they never saw her again. They finally placed a small mound of stones high on the bank of the river where they thought she had last stood. Maybe it would serve as a beacon to guide her spirit home. Eventually they gave up, and departed in sorrow.

The effigy of the hawk remained hidden in its secret place. It would not be found for many years. The mound of stones eventually collapsed as the river became a stream, and then a mere seasonal trickle of water. Once every few years the trickle would swell to a flood as if remembering what it once had been, but it was a parody of its former self. Men came and went—strange men who had forgotten the important things that had once happened here. The world became a different place. But the hawk effigy knew, and remembered. Years passed and times changed, but hawk kept vigil.

The little girl was not conscious of the passing of time, but she was somehow troubled. She didn't quite know what had happened to her and she had many questions. She felt the same, but somehow different. Her surroundings seemed somewhat gray, as if the sun was hidden from her view. It was not really unpleasant, but she didn't know what to do next.

She thought it best to stay where she was and wait for help—for guidance. This place was familiar, somehow, but seemed different than she remembered.

Then one day she felt a calling, a tugging that guided her to the last place she remembered on Earth. Although the mound of stones up on the hill had long since disappeared, there was a new circle of stones placed below, ringing in the place of power that had beckoned her long ago and caused her to walk too close to the edge of the river. She was fascinated by the wheel of stones, and approached it with pent-up anticipation.

It was here that she saw the spirit guide. He was a kindly man with a white beard who recognized her immediately and called her "ancestor." He held out his hands and invited her to dance. At first they just held hands and twirled around with no pattern and no ritual. But it was joyous. Then he asked her to teach him to dance the way she was accustomed. She began to show him the dance steps used by her family on special occasions—celebrations of good things. Together they danced round and round the circle. As they danced the gray began to lift. She began to awaken as if from a long sleep. She looked up toward the side of the stream where she had last stood, where the mound of stones marking her passing had been placed. A strange structure now stood there, rising up far above her.

And there stood her family! They greeted her as if she had returned from a journey! She was reunited with those whom she loved. The skies cleared above her and all was bright and blue and gold.

Below her the spirit guide ceased his dance and slowly faded away. For a moment it was as if she had been contained within an immense universe of love. And then that universe in turn filled her to overflowing.

Far above, Hawk looked down and smiled. All that had been needed was time. And time meant nothing, really. It was all an illusion. But a very pleasant one as such.

What does all this mean? I've had years now to consider the possibilities. Did I imagine the whole thing? Did I string together thoughts and images, dreams and daydreams, to weave a completely imaginary fabric of illusion that, for some reason, I want to believe?

My problem with this simple but obvious explanation is that on many levels I *don't* want to believe it really happened, in this or any other universe. If it did, and if I accept it, that means much of my life has been spent living a lie. For most of my professional life I simply did not believe in such things. I even privately looked askance at those who did. In fact, there is a very big part of me that still refuses to believe it is possible for everyday people like me to see into hidden dimensions and time zones, all of which must be real if this story is true. It would be much easier to retire into the sunset and die a peaceful death after a successful life well spent.

But I can't. The images are too real. The experience too vivid. My study of metaphysics, although certainly not academically certified, has produced too many questions to doubt the validity of the possibility of such things.

And there's one more thing. It might sound silly, but I can't ignore it.

A few years ago my wife, Barbara, was looking for stones to build a fence. She was searching along a natural shoreline that once would have been part of an ancient tributary of the Savannah River. This would have been the beach of that ancient lake that covered the ground where our Medicine Wheel is now located. We built our gazebo right at the high water mark. It's a good place to look for material that would make a dandy stone wall.

One of the stones she found was palm sized, obviously worked by an ancient hand, and felt warm to the touch.

It appeared to have been shaped into the image of a hawk.

TWO
MOVING OUT OF BODY IN FULL CONSCIOUSNESS

"The scientific recognition of the multidimensional universe and the continuum of consciousness is the primary missing element in our comprehension of the unseen nature and structure of all energy throughout the universe."
William Buhlman in *Adventures Beyond the Body*

"Out" of Body?

What do we mean when we say we go "out" of body? Do we actually leave our material structure behind? Is there such a thing as an "astral" body? What leaves? Where does it go? What's really going on during an OBE?

These are difficult questions which, quite truthfully, no one can probably answer with a great deal of certainty. There are many books and articles written on the subject, but after you read enough of them and compare what others say to your own experiences, questions remain, along with the nagging suspicion that there are as many competing camps in the OBE world as there are denominations in the Christian Church. Similar to the current state of organized religion, there may be out-of-body solidarity when it comes to the overall premise, but there are differing opinions about the best way to proceed.

If we are going to make progress toward our goal of perceiving other realities we have to begin at the beginning and honestly face up to the task ahead. Acting on faith alone doesn't cut it. Intellect and intuition must go hand in hand. When it comes to understanding the nature of OBEs, we need to see clearly what we are facing and refuse to leave our intelligence behind at the door. Otherwise we are only fooling ourselves. If OBEs constitute a scientific event as well as a metaphysical phenomenon, they will stand up to scrutiny. Indeed, they *must* stand up to scrutiny or they are not worthy of our study.

What's really going on when we seem to go "out" of body? In this chapter we'll try to get a handle on the subject.

Astral Body Theory

Probably the most accepted theory held by those who study Out-of-Body Experiences, both OBEs and NDEs (Near-Death Experiences), is that our essence is housed in both a physical body and what is often called an astral body, or a non-physical body. People often report seeing themselves as young, in good shape, strong, and healthy. They also report seeing loved ones not as they looked when they died, but appearing as if they were in the prime of life.

This is the accepted theory behind ghosts and spectral entities as well. Such astral beings are often thought to be "stuck" in this world, tied down by their still-existing habit of identifying too closely with life on this physical plane.

The word astral, used in this context, refers to a non-physical realm of existence somehow connected to its physical counterpart. It's real. It's just not material, or composed of atoms and cellular structure. Although this theory was embraced and publicized by Theosophists more than one hundred years ago, there appears to be ancient textual support for it as well, based on an enigmatic verse written by an anonymous author in the book of Ecclesiastes:

> "Remember your creator in the days of your youth ... before the silver cord is broken ... and the dust returns to the earth as it was, and (your) breath returns to God who gave it."
>
> Ecclesiastes 12:6

From this verse arose the belief that the astral and physical bodies are connected by a proverbial "silver cord." Many who have OBEs claim to have seen this cord. Presumably at death it is broken, thus our connection with the physical plane is severed and we go wherever it is we are destined to go. It's this "astral" body that gave birth to the term Astral Travel.

Etheric Travel

Astral Travel, however, is often confused with the term *Etheric Travel*. There is a subtle difference between them. Technically, travel within our physical plane and time while out of body is called Etheric Travel. Astral Travel includes experiencing different times and different planes of existence, some of which appear to be extremely foreign to anything experienced on earth.

Robert Monroe explained the differentiation quite clearly. He often said that Etheric Travel took place in what he called "Local 1" or the "Here/Now." In this type of experience, out-of-body travelers relate to people and places that actually exist, right now. This is why volunteers from the military were sent to the Monroe Institute to study remote viewing. The army wanted to know if it was possible to spy on enemies in real time from the secure comfort of one's own living room.

Consider, for example, this entry from my journal, which illustrates the concept of Etheric Travel out of body:

August 11, 2014

Suddenly I found myself, completely unexpectedly, on Martha's Vineyard in Massachusetts, trying to talk to the President of the United States. He seemed as close to me as if we were both in the same room. My wife used to live on Martha's Vineyard and I've visited a few times. When she later asked me if I recognized any buildings, I drew a complete blank. I have no idea why I "knew" I was there. Later, as a matter of fact, I remember thinking that I must have been mistaken. I assumed that with all the current tension in the Middle East, President Obama must be in Washington. But, as it turned out, he was there on the Vineyard at the time, doing whatever passes for a presidential vacation, assuming that there is such a thing. I seem to remember that I had a message that needed to be delivered to him. The message was: "Faith, trust, and belief." That's all. But I said it a few times and he seemed to nod, as if hearing the words.

When I returned to my body I wondered if someone had given him a copy of the book I had written with that title. My ego thus reared its ugly head. But at the time, I wasn't interested in him thinking of me at all. I just felt that in the midst of all the turmoil he was experiencing he needed to be grounded in faith, trust, and belief. That's all.

Later: It turns out someone did eventually send him a copy of my book, Faith, Trust & Belief. *I did! He and Michelle sent me a nice thank you letter. It was a form letter, of course, but I really appreciated it.*

Notice the here/now aspects of this story. Although I couldn't recognize any buildings in a place I have visited half a dozen times, I somehow knew I was on Martha's Vineyard. That is a real place. Although I didn't know at the time that the president and his family were there on vacation, I saw him there in real time.

In other words, there was no exotic locale or shift of time sequence. Everything happened in the current space-time continuum. If I indeed journeyed to Martha's Vineyard, assuming I didn't imagine the whole thing, then that's an example of Etheric Travel.

Astral Travel

Shamanic practitioners are more familiar with Astral Travel, reporting that they go to strange-appearing worlds that exist parallel to this one and separate from our concept of time. As an example, here's another journal entry:

July, 2013

After about a half hour of listening to music I feel very relaxed. Even if nothing "happens" during a time of meditation I find it very restful.

Just before I decide it's time to open my eyes, however, I sense a shift occurring. I am taken completely by surprise. Something very powerful seems to be surrounding and overwhelming me and I am almost frightened by the feeling of helplessness it engenders.

But curiosity triumphs over fright. That's a good thing, because I have never had a bad experience while meditating and I really don't feel there is ever any need to fear. Perhaps "anticipation" is a better word. There is a feeling that I am about to jump off a diving board into the deep end of the pool. Afterward, waking doubts are almost always present—"Am I just making this up?" But when I am in the moment there is no doubt at all that this is the real thing, and it's bigger than anything life has to offer.

Suddenly I am aware that before me are many, many totem spirit creatures—far too many to count. It's as if they are all dancing or whirling around together, caught in an immense vortex. The colors are the colors of nature—greens and browns, blacks and tans—but all swirling around until they mix together like paint in a bucket and merge into one huge, powerful, green, gold and silver, fire-breathing dragon. That's right, a dragon! It's the first time I've ever seen one in a vision like this.

I suppose I should be frightened, but I'm not—even when in the next moment I am riding the dragon just as Harry Potter might have. Up, up we go, until the earth below is only a soft, green vision. All of a sudden I am conscious that a familiar gate I have often seen in vision is now far below. Up until now it's always been either a barricade or stepping-off point. I've rarely gone through it. But now I view it as if flying over it in an airplane. The dragon even banks to the left to give me a better view. There is no stopping to peek across this time! We simply fly right over it until it seems to be only a speck in the distance.

What lies before us is an immense field of gray, silver, and white. It is perfectly flat but, at the same time, seems to have waves upon waves rippling across its surface. It seems soft and comforting, but infinite in size. It just goes on and on forever. The dragon flies down closer until we are almost skimming across its surface.

In thought, I ask the dragon to drop me off here—to simply roll over and let me tumble down to the surface. But the dragon answers, "No, that is something you must do yourself!"

And I do! I just jump off, not knowing what to expect.

What happens is beyond my ability to adequately describe, but I'll try. It seems, somehow, that all my fears and anxieties, all my guilt, doubts, and embarrassments, all my misguided hopes and aspirations, are absorbed into the field of gray and white. They disappear—and I'm left bouncing on the surface as if it's a great big trampoline. I'm like a kid again. I have never before in my life experienced such unmitigated joy. Bouncing up and down, doing jumps and spins, inscribing great arcs and flips. Never have I had such fun!

Next thing I know, I'm back home in my chair with a silly grin on my face.

For those who recall a similar scene from the movie, Harry Potter and the Deathly Hollows: Part 2, *and wonder if it influenced me, I need to point out that although the movie was released two years before my OBE, I didn't see it until the year after I had the experience. It was still fresh enough in my mind so that I could smile to myself when I saw Harry and his intrepid friends acting out my ride. As Yogi Berra would say, it was like déjà vu all over again!*

Notice the differences between these two OBEs. Dragons, obviously, don't exist in physical reality. The landscape as well appears to be totally foreign to our perception realm. Time had ceased. Whatever this experience was, it certainly didn't consist of real events in real time. This is the kind of reality experienced in Astral Travel.

Problems Arise

A lot more could be said on this subject, but the end result is that those who describe OBEs in terms of Astral or Etheric travel postulate a non-physical body that may or may not be connected to our physical body. It is this astral body that moves to either actual locations and times or parallel realities. This is the body that seems to move "out" in an OBE. Often this explanation is accompanied by the theory that although our two bodies, physical and astral, share similarities, they differ in their vibrational frequencies.

But there are problems with this theory, and they involve our physical conception of body and brain. Simply put, the intriguing "I" rears its head again. Who, or what, is the "I" that "has" an astral body? Or is the astral body itself the illusive "I" that "has" a temporary physical body which is discarded at death?

Once we start to think in these terms we lock ourselves into the whole concept of form. We begin to think in terms of human-ness, either physical or astral, as a necessary form for consciousness.

What if that's not the case at all? What if something quite different is happening? Could it be that our brains are interpreting something, in the only way they can, that is totally outside of our imagination? In other words, if our consciousness *is* able to bypass our senses and interact with a world outside our perception realm, the only way we could possibly make any sense of the whole experience is to frame it in images that we *do* understand. If this is the case, our brains are doing what they have evolved to do. They observe, organize, and create understandable images so we can relate to an unfamiliar experience.

Was I really riding a dragon? Of course not. But out of the entire rolodex of life events I have amassed, either experienced, visualized, or imagined, that was the one that my brain selected to best describe what I was experiencing. In other words, I wasn't riding a dragon, but that was what it *seemed* like. Did I bounce around on some foreign field of cloud-like reality? No, but that's what it *felt* like.

New Theory

If all this is true, then maybe the time has come to re-think our entire notion of OBEs. Maybe the term even needs to be changed. Perhaps we don't *go* anywhere at all. Maybe, instead, we simply glimpse a reality outside our usual perception realm. But the only way our earth-bound brains can express the experience is to couch it in terms that are familiar enough for us to understand.

That may explain NDEs as well. When our consciousness separates at death we still exist in an eternal state and experience the now-familiar stages of a tunnel of light, spirit guides, and a life review. When our brains are revived, they then go back to doing what they do so well—organizing and interpreting what our eternal consciousness experienced in the interim.

Here's where quantum theorists can help us. Over the last hundred years they have developed a keen ability to think outside the box about realities that are real but whacky—counter intuitive but scientifically verifiable.

One such concept is called non-locality. Hold on to your hats for this one. It's so weird that even Albert Einstein refused to accept it at first. For a long time he called it "spooky action at a distance." Here's why.

Einstein had determined that nothing in nature can move faster than the speed of light. In his cosmos, everything performed like billiard balls on a pool table. It was pure, unadulterated, classical physics. If the 8-ball was struck by the cue ball, it caused a measurable and predictable reaction. Furthermore, if the 8-ball even wanted to pass information on to the cue ball, that information could only travel at the speed of light. So if Captain Kirk out in space wanted to communicate with Mr. Spock back on the Starship Enterprise, his message could travel no faster than the speed of light, no matter what kind of "sub-space frequencies" the sci-fi writers decided to invent. It takes a long time for a message to travel out into distant space and then return, as all the scientists at NASA learn when they send a message to the Jupiter space probe.

But physicists have now discovered that in the quantum world, the world of the ultra small, that truism simply doesn't apply. Non-locality describes a totally counter-intuitive reality. The truth is that down deep in the underlying structure of the cosmos, sub-atomic particles are able to instantly communicate with one another no matter where they happen to be at the time.

How? No one knows. But it has been proven time and time again. Apparently both particles exist as part of a field in which all things are instantly and simultaneously connected. Spin a particle clockwise over *here* and its entangled twin will immediately spin counter-clockwise over *there*, no matter how far apart they may be.

It's weird, but it's true. Even Einstein was eventually won over.

Here's the point. If this kind of thing goes on at the quantum level, could it also occur at the level of human consciousness? In other words, could out-of-body travel consist of moving out from under the tyranny of the five senses in order to become instantly aware of all things, everywhere? Might this happen without any "movement" at all? Could it be that such "trips" don't involve a "body," astral or not, "going" somewhere as much as it means a shift of awareness, after which our brains try to make sense of what happened by imaging a "body" that "went" somewhere? When we recall the experience, even moments after it happens, we picture a trip—an excursion. But what really happened was that for a few minutes our consciousness simply expanded into the reality which surrounds us.

Now, think about what this means. During an OBE you feel that everything is real. It seems more vivid than the reality you live in, day to day. And it is! Your normal life consists of deciphering an illusion produced by your five senses. Of course an OBE is going to *feel* more real than that.

But when you "return" to your senses, they will immediately convince you that what you experienced while "out" was just in your head.

How could it be otherwise? Your memory of that trip is interpreted by your physical brain, which will select past experiences to produce an image of what just happened in order to make sense of it. But by the time that takes place you are *remembering* something, not *experiencing* it.

This is extremely important. When you experience an out-of-body journey, try to remember what it felt like *at the time*, not what you thought about it after it happened. *Afterwards* is just a memory recalled through the normal, neural process of a physical brain that will someday decay and die. What's important is the *now* experience. Trust it!

No wonder so many people come back from an OBE and say, "It felt so real!" It was!

So—What Happened?

What does all this mean? Simply this. It really doesn't matter what physically happens during an OBE. Perhaps there *is* an astral body that travels to parallel plains or dimensions. But maybe there isn't. Perhaps the astral body you imagine is just a mental construct thought up by a physical brain trying to make sense of an experience that is totally different from anything you have previously encountered.

In the end, who cares? The experience you have while in the illusive "Now," the eternal stillness which you will someday know when you die, is the important thing.

Is it all in your head?

Well, the memory of it certainly is. The interpretations formed by the neural processes of the brain make it seem that way.

But don't forget this important fact. Someday those neural processes will cease. We call it being "brain-dead." And all the illusions they produced will die with them.

So—are you going to believe a message stored in the electrical neural networks of a physical blob of cellular protoplasm, or in an experience that seemed vivid and eternal while it was going on in the eternal now? Are you going to accept the Great Illusion or an actual experience of an eternal reality?

We may never be able to figure out the physics of Astral Travel, Etheric Travel, Remote Viewing, Shamanic Journeying, or Out-of-Body Experience. During this life we will probably never know what we "look like" apart from our physical bodies. It may turn out that such things are so foreign to our senses that we can't even imagine them. The illuminating views, the splendor, the vivid colors and heavenly sounds we experience during an OBE might prove to be, at best, a pale memory of their reality. As long as we are slaves to our physical brains, neural pathways, and fuzzy recall, we just won't know.

So maybe it's best to listen to the words of the Apostle Paul, the author of almost a third of the New Testament in the Bible, and, according to the lines of II Corinthians 12:2, no stranger to OBEs himself:

"Eye hath not seen, nor ear heard, neither have entered into the heart of [anyone], the things which God hath prepared..."

I Corinthians 2:9

Is This For Real?

To get a handle on the science behind all this we need to turn to the work of a man who has written extensively about the whole idea of consciousness. His name is Ervin Lazlo.

Lazlo, combining math, science, religion, and the tools of both the physicist and philosopher, describes a field consisting of what he calls "in-formation." By that he means a field that is in the process of being "formed" as it catalogues our experience. It is a place, for lack of a better word, from which all energy comes into existence and to which all matter eventually returns. Because it is the source of all matter it absolutely enthralls scientists at CERN's Large Hadron Collider in Switzerland.

Both Einstein and Stephen Hawking felt the need to turn to religious language when they referred to this field as the "mind of God." It is both the originator and receiver of particles that spring into existence from "nowhere" and go back to "somewhere" just as quickly, passing through the newly discovered Higgs Field, the field that enables energy to take on mass and collapse into matter.

Lazlo, too, utilizes religious language. But he borrows from the ancient, spiritual, language of Sanskrit when he calls it *Akasha*.

Akasha means "space." According to Lazlo, the *Akashic Field* is a "quantum vacuum" that supports not only fundamental energy but, more important still, also the bits of information that manifest themselves in what we call material objects. And he goes further than that. He believes the Akashic Field supports not only this Cosmos, this universe, but all universes, past and present, discovered and undiscovered. In other words, he is talking about a field that supports the Multiverse.

Akasha is thus the mysterious realm from which everything originates—an infinite wave of potential awaiting incarnation in matter. Every symphony Mozart wrote, every painting daVinci created, every possible outcome to any choice you ever made, every idea you ever had—all existed in potential in Akasha. When Mozart, daVinci, or you, plucked an idea out of Akasha, it was given life through your intention. Akasha is the home of the Muse, but much, much more. It is the Source, the Ground of Being. It is Consciousness itself.

In the world of quantum physics, nothing comes into existence until someone measures it. A probability wave of potential does not collapse into matter until we give it our attention.

That describes Akasha. There, everything exists in potential but it manifests itself only when we choose to collapse it into our existence. According to a popular theory put forth by Hugh Everett way back in 1951, the moment you choose a particular manifestation, thereby bringing it into our universe, another "you" somewhere in the infinite Multiverse chooses another possible manifestation, until all potential possibilities are manifested somewhere, somehow.

The Source of Our Current Knowledge

This is difficult stuff. But remember that these theories don't come from mystics and those who study metaphysics. They arise out of the complex mathematics of theoretical physicists. You don't even have to read exotic ancient texts or modern textbooks about quantum physics to learn about them. Just turn on *Through the Wormhole* with actor Morgan Freeman or some other contemporary program on the Science Channel, USA.

If you are skeptical about all this, I understand. Most days, I am, too. But here's how it relates to OBEs. We know that we are dependent on our five senses. They've become a part of our reality. They have even shaped how we think about our existence. Most of us can't imagine a reality that doesn't conform to our sensory perceptions.

Up to now, these senses have been very reliable. But they don't work out there in the Field of Akasha.

Deepak Chopra, in his book, *Life After Death*, describes consciousness as being a kind of three-layer cake. The top layer is the dimension of physical matter, the world of concrete objects we encounter through the five senses. This is the layer that scientists observe and measure, quantify and study.

Beneath that is the dimension of subtle objects. This is the world of dreams and visions, imagination and inspiration.

Underlying it all is the dimension of pure Consciousness itself, the field of Akasha. That is the mysterious realm that gives birth to everything there is. It is the ground of our being. It is Consciousness becoming aware of itself.

When we bypass our senses and somehow personally connect with this field, we become, in the words of Zen Buddhism, one with everything. Whether or not there is some kind of "body" that travels to this realm, we are, in every practical sense of the word, "out" of body.

Perhaps these words from Sir Arthur Eddington best capture the whole idea:

"The universe is not only stranger than we imagine; it is stranger than we can imagine."

Assuming, then, that we can get "out there," wherever "there" is, what will we find? What might we encounter?

That's where we'll turn next.

THREE
SPIRIT GUIDES AND HELPERS

"An angel of the Lord appeared to them ... and they were terrified."
Luke 2:9

Visitors From Beyond

If you are interested in the historical records of people who have interacted with spirit guides or helpers from outside our perception realm, you need look no further than the pages of the Bible. This story touches all the bases:

"In the year that King Uzziah died, I saw the Lord, high and exalted, seated on a throne; and the train of his robe filled the temple. Above him were seraphim, each with six wings: With two wings they covered their faces, with two they covered their feet, and with two they were flying. And they were calling to one another:

'Holy, holy, holy is the Lord Almighty; the whole earth is full of his glory.'

At the sound of their voices the doorposts and thresholds shook and the temple was filled with smoke.

'Woe to me!' I cried. 'I am ruined! For I am a man of unclean lips, and I live among a people of unclean lips, and my eyes have seen the King, the Lord Almighty.'

Then one of the seraphim flew to me with a live coal in his hand, which he had taken with tongs from the altar. With it he touched my mouth and said, 'See, this has touched your lips; your guilt is taken away and your sin atoned for.'

Then I heard the voice of the Lord saying, 'Whom shall I send? And who will go for us?'

And I said, 'Here am I. Send me!'"

Isaiah 6:1-8

Notice the key points:

- Isaiah is a prophet—a holy man. In other words, he is a shaman.
- He yearns to bring peace and solace to his tribe, which is undergoing difficult times. Their king has just died and their future looks bleak.
- In the midst of an OBE he experiences an astral journey, finding himself in an unanticipated and completely foreign environment.
- There he meets strange winged creatures who appear to be part human, part bird.
- Upon acknowledging his smallness and inadequacy in the midst of such a place, he undergoes a shamanic initiation. What appear to be live coals are placed on his lips but he experiences no pain.
- He comes to understand that what appears to be a supernatural entity desires an earthly messenger for the purpose of promoting healing to his tribe.
- He volunteers for the job and returns with information that precipitates cultural revolution.

This is nothing less than a description of a typical shamanic out-of-body journey. Were it not found in a revered text layered over by thousands of years of religious indoctrination, it would be perfectly obvious to anyone.

As things stand today, however, to suggest such a thing in most churches, temples, and mosques is to risk expulsion and accusations of heresy.

The venerated prophet Isaiah, a shaman? A description of an OBE in the Bible? Bible stories equated with pagan traditions? Never!

But there it is, in black and white, straight from the pages of Holy Writ.

Israel, at that time, needed help. Isaiah wanted to be an instrument of healing. The cosmos provided a Spirit Guide.

Thus it always seems to be. If we are open, help is sent, often in a completely unexpected way. That's what happened to me. My story is not as dramatic as Isaiah's, but it's certainly as applicable to the subject of guides and helpers.

The Nude Woman on the Rock

Many years ago I was a Christian fundamentalist. Now, you have to understand something about fundamentalists, whether they are religious, political, social or philosophical in nature. Whenever you meet someone who claims to know THE TRUTH, you can safely assume two things. First of all, they don't. Second, they're probably obnoxious.

All religions breed fundamentalists. Political parties and scientific communities do it, too. Someone gets to be an expert, gathers a following and then, suddenly, a fundamentalist is born. This is the person who knows it all, at least as "it" pertains to his or her own body of knowledge. They determine the fundamentals, the things you simply have to believe if you are going to be in their group. Those who accept the fundamentals are "sound." They can be trusted. They teach their system to others, who probably do not completely understand everything. But they believe in the leader, so they go along.

There was a time when I had such a following. I had a radio show, was speaking at various churches and civic groups about different religious topics, and believed that the earth was only 6,000 years old. I could support that belief with many different Scripture verses and could be very obnoxious at parties and social gatherings.

I now freely confess—I thought I knew most of the answers. I was a Christian fundamentalist, through and through. I bought and taught the whole party line. Although I am no longer a fundamentalist I still consider myself a Christian, but for a while I walked a pretty tight rope, and even came within a hair's breadth of falling off. Here's what happened.

My Christian label back then was New England Congregationalist. We were descended from good Puritan stock. Perhaps "stocks" would be a better name, given the puritanical penchant for punishing protagonist perpetrators. (Somebody once described a Puritan as someone who suffered from the fear that somewhere in the world, someone might be happy.)

Things have changed somewhat since Puritan times. As a matter of fact, the United Church of Christ, my denomination, is descended in part from Puritan roots but has the reputation of being very liberal. Back then, though, I wasn't. The more I studied the Bible and built my intellectual systematic theology on what I considered to be its inerrant texts, the more I came to believe that I was preaching *THE TRUTH!*

It made perfect sense to me, then, that the church in the next town, since they didn't agree with me, wasn't preaching the truth. Since my way was God's way—after all, it came straight from the Bible—then they must be wrong. If they were wrong, they must be deceived. If they were deceived, they must not be of God.

See how it works?

Okay, it probably sounds silly to you. Maybe even dangerous. But I'll bet you have some of your own ideas, either religious or political, wherein you feel like a true believer while knowing in your heart of hearts that your Uncle Fred is dead wrong. (By the way, the older we get, the harder it is to avoid the trap.)

Fundamentalists are not very tolerant. "Those who are not with us are against us!" That kind of thing. Even presidents say it. It's pretty common.

What made this whole philosophical structure fall apart was the fact that one day I risked being open enough to consider what was, to me at least, a heretical idea as I sat at my desk putting together a sermon about a topic I have long since forgotten. I do remember that it seemed very important at the time. Following my usual *modus operandi* I was compiling Biblical proof texts right and left, selecting from here and there and arranging them in some kind of order while imagining myself metaphorically bludgeoning an audience over the head with incontrovertible evidence.

A nagging thought kept pestering me, though, one that I had dimly noticed for some time but had successfully managed to keep safely at bay. It had been crouching in the shrubbery of my mind, like a hungry lion waiting to pounce. Finally it did.

You see, I had, for many years, been studying the Bible in more depth than most people ever bother to do. I knew it backwards and forwards. I knew how Romans related to Genesis and Revelation related to Isaiah. I saw it as one long story.

But the very fact of my familiarity became the problem. When it came to content, the Bible held no secrets from me. We were like an old married couple who knew each other's strengths and weaknesses, so I was very much aware that there were troubling texts that seemed contradictory, inaccurate, or downright wrong. I had learned how to skirt around those portions, pretending they didn't exist. I had become similar to a lawyer, arguing in defense of a client I secretly knew was guilty. When I finally opened myself up to admitting it, there in the privacy of my lonely office, it led to my downfall.

Put simply, the bottom line was this: Over the years I had come to base my entire theology on Biblical proof texts. Now, what if it could be demonstrated to my satisfaction that the Bible was not without what I would call error? What if that wonderful collection of wisdom and inspiration even contained some discrepancies or historical inaccuracies? Worse yet, what if the original authors never intended their work to be considered inerrant? In other words, what if the modern doctrine of inerrancy was something I was superimposing on documents meant to be understood in quite a different way?

Do you see the problem? If an argument about the existence of God hinges on proof texts selected from a Bible that is said to be without error, then all someone has to do is show that the Bible contains some discrepancies and the argument is over. God simply ceases to exist. In other words, I wasn't preaching about God anymore. I was preaching about an inerrant, infallible Bible. In my theology, the Bible had taken the place of God.

Clearly I had a problem. My whole faith system was shaken to the core. Everything I believed was suddenly called into question. All the stuff I had studied in seminary about genuine, historical criticism of the Bible came back to haunt me. I couldn't ignore it anymore.

At that moment, I decided I would have to leave the ministry and go back to teaching music. I was completely devastated. I no longer had anything to say from the pulpit.

Right then I decided to go on retreat for a few days. I had built a small log cabin up in New Hampshire, so I decided to go up there for a while, be alone, and see if I could find some kind of answer.

While I was there I encountered an opportunity for openness.

Three days into my lonely retreat I hiked up a mountain that I had climbed a dozen times before. It exactly suited my needs because it was high enough to be a challenge but, when you got to the top, opened up to a magnificent view of miles and miles of countryside. Most important—I had never seen anybody else up there.

Today was different. Topping the last rise, discouraged and completely at odds with myself, lost in the terribly despondent throes of a real mid-life crisis and a dark night of the soul, I came out of the trees and met, face to face so to speak, a nude woman sunbathing on a rock.

Nothing in the world is more threatening to a true-blue fundamentalist preacher than a nude woman on a rock, surrounded by nature. Isis unbound! At first glance she represented everything that was foreign to my way of thinking. She looked primitive, pagan, sinful, and worst of all, absolutely free.

Fundamentalists have an unhealthy fear of too much freedom.

I turned to walk away, averting my eyes from such unbridled sinfulness as a naked human body. But before I could take more than a step or two, she yelled, "Hi! Come on over and join me."

What could I do? I mean, I was up there in front of God and everybody, fearfully certain that my entire congregation was momentarily going to step out of the woods in condemnation, and this woman, rather than covering up, was inviting me to join her.

Now, how does a man say no to a nude woman on a rock? Every instinct, every one, said, "Get out of here! You remember what happened to Joseph back in the book of Genesis. He got set up and paid the price! This is definitely, most definitely, the work of the devil. Flee for your life!"

But somehow I found myself sitting down and talking to her. We talked about everything from reincarnation to crystals, from meditation to out-of-body travel. She was interested, really interested, in what I believed and why

I believed it. I was fascinated by what she had to say. I had, until then, been utterly opposed to those I called worldly people. But here I was, sitting right next to a living, breathing, nude, worldly person, who wanted to learn more about spiritual information.

Know what? So did I. Sometime during that long afternoon I realized I was having the first really spirited and spiritual conversation I had had in a long time. A philosophical vista opened before me. Here we were—two seekers on different paths—each looking for the same thing—sharing our insights on the journey—helping a fellow traveler along the way.

To this day, I believe God, whoever He/She/It may be, has a tremendous sense of humor. I can't think of a better way to knock a fundamentalist over the head than by taking him up a mountain, just like Moses, and then, instead of giving him the Ten Commandments, introducing him to a nude woman on a rock.

There was absolutely nothing sexual about the meeting. (Well, maybe a little at first—but only for a moment and only in my mind. I may have been a fundamentalist, but I wasn't dead.) It was a meeting of souls, not bodies. But at the end of our time, when we both went our separate ways, I said to her, "You know, I don't even know your name."

"Does it matter?" she asked, and we both laughed. It didn't matter. What mattered was that we met when we needed to meet and both left the mountain changed. I didn't give up anything that day. I found something. I am still a Christian, but a very different kind. My religion has more than enough mystery for me to understand, or even explore sufficiently, in my lifetime. So now I like to talk to people from other traditions, people who can teach me something. I'm not nearly so quick to judge. We are, all of us, in the words of my tradition, children of God.

Spirit Guides

But help can come from other places as well. I have no doubt that the woman I met that day was a flesh and blood, warm and breathing, real, live person, although a few people with whom I shared this story over the years tried to convince me that I might have experienced a supernatural entity.

Lately, however, I *have* had occasion to be in the presence of quite a different kind of spirit guide. Consider these entries from my journal:

August 9, 2012

While in the midst of a deep meditation this evening I was taken by surprise—totally out of left field.

I seemed to float out of my body and move out to the front porch. There I mentally picked up an ancient stone Savannah River projectile point that Barb had recently found while planting a rose bush in the front yard. As I held it in my hand a sharp emotional pain went through me. Up until ten years ago I was an avid hunter. There were times when my family almost lived on wild game. But suddenly I realized that this beautiful object was meant to hurt, wound, and destroy either a game animal or another person. The pain seemed so sharp I felt for a moment that it might have once killed someone. I felt as though perhaps, in a previous incarnation, I had once even used it to take life. I felt like crying.

Then, out of a misty shape before me, came two hands that cupped mine as I held the spear point in my own hands. I "heard" a voice saying, "It's all right—It's all right." I immediately felt comforted, and the hands held mine for the rest of the meditation. I didn't want it to end. I felt as though my higher self was holding my hands and reassuring me.

It was wonderful. When the music ended and my meditation was over, I didn't want to come back!

I have since met this presence, this spirit guide, many, many times. Over the course of nine years he has rarely failed to be there for me. I even gave him a name. I couldn't get the name *Sobuko* out of my head. Although I have searched and searched I can't find its meaning. It just seems to be a name that materialized out of the blue.

I used to ask why. I wondered time and time again if this was an actual spiritual entity who inhabited a parallel dimension. If so, presumably he had better things to do than hang around waiting for me to contact him. The whole thing seemed a bit bizarre and totally out of character for me. I once quietly scoffed at people who made such claims. But almost every time I meditate and engage in an OBE, there he is again, usually standing about two feet off to my left. He rarely smiles, and appears to have American Indian features—shoulder-length straight hair, high cheek bones and a longish, serious face. For some reason, I haven't the foggiest idea what kind of clothes he wears. He appears to be dressed, but for the life of me I don't know in what, and I've really tried to notice.

Although I'll have much more to say later about this entity who now seems closer than a brother to me, I have come to the tentative conclusion that he is me—my higher self. His actual appearance is probably beyond my comprehension. We tend to think in anthropomorphic terms. But out of all the possible forms he could take, this is the one my brain seems to have chosen that allows my conscious self to identify him. He might have taken the form of a fairy or elf. Perhaps I could have visualized him as a beam of light or an animal. But, probably because of my life-long identification with American Indian cultures, this is what works for me.

In other words, I have come to believe Sobuko is me on the "other side," as it were—the source of all lives, past and present, that "I" have ever lived in this and every other alternate universe. If that is true, and if, as we shall later see, quantum theory holds true, Sobuko could very well be the unifying observer of his various selves as they inhabit different, parallel universes, gathering the experience that will bring him to perfection.

I tend to think that this physical body is my only identity, of course. My senses can't wrap themselves around the idea that there may be multiple universes out there, each unique to itself. (Hold on to the thought about quantum theory and the Observer Effect. We'll return to it later. For now it's enough to know that although the universe is much bigger than we can really imagine, there is always help available.)

This leads us to another entry from my OBE journal:

August 11, 2014

For some time now I have been suffering from a severe depression. It almost has me paralyzed. I've been chalking it up to the hot, humid weather. I don't want to do anything except read spiritual material. I was obsessed with the futility of life. Everything seemed pointless and Barb and I have discussed the theory that, in the words of the Buddha, "All life is suffering." To quote Quoheleth in Ecclesiastes, "Meaningless . . . All is Meaningless!" In other words, this material life could very well be hell itself. If a definition of Hell is "separation from God," and our senses envelope us, creating a sense of separation, then the definition sure fits. With that as a background, I awoke at 5:00 this morning with a vivid dream echoing in my head.

The Dream

I was shopping for screen doors at either Lowe's or Home Depot. The colors of the store kept changing from one to the other so I assume the "where" isn't important. What matters is the fact that I was looking for doors. I checked out samples in various material, some metal, others wood, and carefully measured them. I finally selected one made of wood that was a standard 36" x 80." After I picked it out I found myself downstairs, in a basement level. I needed to carry the door upstairs. The stairway seemed to be one of those collapsible types that opens from an upstairs trap door, similar to the kind you find mounted in the ceiling to enter an attic. You pull on a rope, the door opens and a stairway comes down that leads to the next floor. But now I was in trouble. I was by far the oldest person in the store, the climb was difficult, and I found myself gasping for breath, sure I was having a heart attack. I struggled on. As I neared the top I was just about at the end of my endurance, feeling sure I was going to die. But people on the next floor (in my memory they seemed to be dressed in white robes, but I can't be certain) reached down for me, lifted me up and laid me out on the floor. I knew I was going to be okay.

The OBE

Now fully awake, but with this scene fresh in my mind, I began to meditate. Almost immediately I found myself out of body, hovering in the room a little to my right and about six feet off the floor, looking down at my body on the chair. I didn't know quite what to do. Even when I try for them, OBEs are unexpected.

I suspected my meditation would now come to an end but I was again surprised. I found myself at a standing stone I had raised a year before. There I knelt on the ground and placed both hands on the stone. I had the impression that Sobuko was kneeling there on the other side, placing his hands over mine. We stood together and he guided me up to the stone circle we had recently discovered at the top of the hill, north of our house.

Again I was surprised. There was a gathering of shamans standing there, ringing the circle. My impression was that there were about fifty of them, and that they had come from some distance, all around, to be there for this ceremony. They were standing still, holding hands in a ring. I expected them to start dancing, and I even tried to get the party going, but they just stood there, welcoming me into their circle. Dancing was not on the agenda today.

After a short time of silence, which was very pleasurable, the two holding my hands suddenly stepped forward and flung me up and out into space. It was like I was being slung out of a slingshot. Up, up and away from the earth. I saw the planets, the sun, and for a brief, terrible (but wonderful) moment, I saw the whole universe. It was similar to a previous OBE I had a few years ago. The whole universe in the palm of my hand!

Then I started back. It was like playing a movie backward, the universe, the sun, the planets and the earth. I was back in the circle with them again. But before I could say anything or thank them, I was back in my body again, in my chair in the living room. I thought that would do it for today, but suddenly became aware that the experience wasn't over yet. I had a strong compulsion to go down to our Medicine Wheel.

Immediately I was there, laying on the ground, totally naked and surrounded by a ring of women. The feminine energy was as strong down here as the masculine energy had been up on the hill. Although I was completely naked and exposed there was no shame, no embarrassment, and no sexual tension, even though I was obviously fully erect. How that could happen with no feeling of sexuality was a mystery to me. This was not some kind of erotic dream. It seemed to be sexuality completely divorced from sex. I don't know how else to explain it. We were involved in some kind of ceremony and I had the impression that sexuality was somehow completely different from my understanding of it—that it was somehow connected to a cosmic power way above human ideas of either pleasure or reproduction. I kept asking for help in understanding what was going on. I had the idea that they understood something that I wanted to know. I felt there was a great mystery here, somehow, and I didn't get it, but wanted to. It was not at all unpleasant. I didn't feel they were keeping secrets from me. I felt more as if they were instructors, trying to teach me something.

This was not some kind of Freudian "naked" or "exposed" dream. All I felt was curiosity. But before I understood, I was back in my body, totally awake and full of adrenalin.

Later that morning I got on my bike and rode for 12 miles, thinking all the way. All I came up with on the ride was that sex/power/magic might be a really cosmic thing. Or not. I just didn't know.

When I came back and told Barb all this she had some insight that sent explosions off in my head. It was her impression that the shamans of the circle and wise women of the Medicine Wheel had given me a gift—that I had passed some kind of test. I had been welcomed both into the shamanic society of men and the society of women. Just as in my dream, I had passed, with great difficulty, through a "door" to the next level and been received and welcomed. I had done the things that needed to be done and was now moving on to the next stage. I'm not a shaman yet, but my training has at least progressed up a level.

Now that I think about it, I have encountered only women and girls down at the Medicine Wheel, and only men on the hilltop circle. Feminine energy, male energy. Interesting. I'm privileged to receive both. This has been a very humbling experience. As always, I'm already impatient for what comes next!

Helpers from Beyond

We come now to the crux, the bottom line, the central point of everything we have been talking about so far. Unless we clear the hurdle we now face, there's no point in going any further.

Here it is, stated in the clearest way possible:

> Do entities from other dimensions exist, and do they sometimes break through to communicate with us?

There it is. If your answer is an unequivocal "yes," you are impatient to continue. If your answer is an equally firm "no," you are probably ready to put down this book and do something else. Statistical evidence has suggested that very rarely will a person change his or her mind from one side to the other. Talking with each other over the divide usually produces only argument.

I want to address, however, the vast number of people who are really on the fence. To you, logic may seem to preclude the existence of ghosts, angels, fairies, leprechauns, and elves, while a tremendous amount of oral history in the form of myth, religious doctrine, and anecdotal stories points to their presence.

What's an educated, down-to-earth, sensible, 21st century person to do?

I completely understand the two sides of the argument. I've been there—in both camps. And I'm not alone. It's an oft-hidden fact that a great many members of today's clergy think about angels, for instance, as a theoretical, doctrinal abstract. Every Christmas we sing, with great gusto, "Hark! The Herald Angels Sing!" We read with loving tenderness that "an angel appeared to Mary" or "the angel of the Lord appeared to Paul." But our modern training makes us feel much more comfortable when we put a good two thousand years between then and now. We keep all such spiritual communication buried deep in the sands of mythological time.

That produces a religious dichotomy, of course. But it allows a modicum of intellectual integrity.

"Do I believe in angelic messengers?" they say. "Sure! But only in theory. Back then, not now."

For those who are not satisfied with this way of handling the problem, it's safe to say that we need a 21st century explanation. Religious texts and mythological folklore offer one line of proof. Is there any evidence from the scientific perspective?

In our generation it has finally become possible to say, "Yes!" From the halls of academia comes a separate line of evidence that points directly to not only the possibility, but also the probability, of extra-dimensional entities, including spirit guides and helpers.

In my book, *Supernatural Gods*, I examined this line of evidence over the course of almost four hundred pages. Obviously we can't go into that kind of detail here. But here's the conclusion I reached after a lot of study, research and direct experimentation.

We do not live in a *Universe*. We live in a *Multiverse*. Theoretical physicists are almost unanimously confident that parallel universes exist which overlap our own. We are separated not by distance, but frequency. And if life has evolved *here*, it almost certainly has evolved *there*. It's probably not biological life as we understand it. But it is life. It is intelligent. It is curious.

Curiosity is the key. If *we* are interested in contacting *them*, *they* are almost certainly interested in contacting *us*.

Our problem is that we don't know how to do it. In our modern world we are inundated with the methods of technology. But technology won't help us contact realms that exist at vibrational frequencies that our telescopes and microscopes can't, by their very nature, penetrate.

The only scientific method we have that comes close is the language of mathematics. This approach is proving very promising. Mathematicians have discovered tantalizing clues built into the very fabric of the universe—clues that seem to say, "We are here!"

This was the central plot device used by the late Carl Sagan in his book *Contact*. He postulated a message placed way downstream in the endless numbers that make up the mysterious numerical constant of pi, the ratio of a circle's diameter to its circumference.

Max Tegmart of MIT, author of the intriguing book, *Our Mathematical Universe: My Quest for the Ultimate Nature of Reality*, wonders if reality itself is based on the language of mathematics.

In April, 2016, Clara Moskowitz wrote an article for *Scientific American* magazine asking if life as we know it might be, in actuality, a highly advanced, mathematically based computer simulation.

Even if these theories ultimately prove to be true, however, they will still fall short in terms of our actually communicating with entities from other dimensions or parallel universes. We might someday learn to send or receive messages such as, "Are you out there?" But we won't ever be able to have a simple conversation or an exchange of philosophical ideas.

To do that we don't need nuts and bolts spaceships or mathematical formulas as much as we need mind melds. We can't travel to these worlds at the speed of light. We need to travel at the speed of thought.

Traveling at the Speed of Thought

Here's where oral history is so important. We haven't always, as a species, been wrapped up in the intellectual baggage of test tubes and microscopes. There have been times in our past when we used quite a different way of relating to the world around us. Powerful religious texts, insightful shamanic methods, mythic stories, and mystic legends tell us, beyond the shadow of a doubt, that there have been times in our past when we marched to the beat of quite a different drummer.

The shamans, mystics, dowsers, seers, and visionaries haven't left us, either. They are still among us. Most are pretty quiet about their presence. After all, who wants to stand up and be ridiculed by the short-sighted skeptics of a so-called "rational" culture?

But they are there. They might even live quietly next door to you. And perhaps the entities who live on the other side of the vibrational fence aren't too far away either. If you can traverse the first symbolic mile away from modern cultural prejudice, they might even be willing to meet you halfway and offer help in your quest for truth.

Consider, for instance, this entry from my journal:

September 14, 2014

I woke up in the middle of the night, feeling wide awake. I decided to meditate in the quiet of early, early morning. Almost right away I felt my consciousness separate from my body and float free. I didn't really know what to do. I tried to move first to our Shaman Circle and then to the Medicine Wheel. Both seemed closed off, but I still felt something very powerful inside me. It was so disconcerting that I almost ended the process right there, but decided to stay with it and empty my mind as much as possible. In short, I just accepted what was happening as a spectator, waiting to see what might happen next.

I found myself standing, perhaps even hovering, over the rock below our back porch, where two lines of earth energy intersect. To my right and down the hill was the feminine energy of the Medicine Wheel. To my left and below me, the masculine energy of our rock spiral. I stood at the intersection of the two, and then turned halfway to my right so that I now faced toward the south, holding out my arms. The Shaman's Circle on the hill above was now on my right, the Medicine Wheel below on my left.

Suddenly, and I do mean suddenly, I was bathed in all the colors of the rainbow. I saw my astral body as if I was standing off to the side while still being present in it. (I'm sorry if that makes no sense, but it's all I can say.)

My feet were rooted to the ground. As a matter of fact, I had no feet. They just plunged into the soil, but my legs consisted of many different colors. It was the same with my head. It was connected to the sky, seemingly turning to colors that just went up and up. (Here I wish I was an artist. Words don't work.)

My arms as well—one disappeared into the colors of the Shaman's Circle, the other into the colors of the Medicine Wheel. I hung suspended in space, a body of rainbow light and color "connected" to the four points of the compass and the four places of power, above and below, left and right. The best I can say is that I "saw" my astral body, consisting of many moving rays of light, suspended in space, connecting spirit above with earth below, and feminine and masculine places of power. I was in the posture of crucifixion, and can only assume that Spirit took the familiar image of the cross to use as a metaphor that I would understand.

I saw a line of male shamans on my right and female shamans on my left, two long, single lines of people, each carrying a goblet (dare I say "grail," or perhaps "cup?") filled with a boiling hot, very frightening, steaming, vial of liquid. They approached me with faces that were resigned but somehow loving. "Tough love," certainly, but loving. They seemed to say, "What must be done will be done."

With that, they began to pour the contents of those hot, boiling, vile, ("sinful" seems to be the word that best fits) goblets of fiery liquid into me. Somehow I wasn't afraid, but waited for the pain to begin.

It never did! It didn't hurt. There was no pain. Instead, I took the dark liquid into myself and somehow transformed it into light. The more they poured, the brighter and more brilliant became the light. It was Alchemy—turning lead into gold. I had, in the words of Christianity, taken into myself the sins of the world, and turned it into glorious light. I had accepted the hurt and pain and turned it into a blessing.

I will never think about biblical crucifixion in the same way again. It's not about a historical event in the past, two thousand years ago. It's not about something that will happen to us when we die in the future. Each one of us, when we made the decision to enter this perception realm, the material world, agreed to "pick up our cross," agreed to be "crucified" by the world. We agreed to take on and accept the pain of life with its humiliation and powerlessness, with its senseless tragedy and futility, and turn it into pure light.

As all this was going on I was very much aware of the place where all opposites crossed. It was right at the juncture of head and feet, left and right arm—the place of my heart chakra.

Although I wanted to stay in this vision forever, there was one more task to accomplish. There was a bit of a party. I was welcomed by both male and female shamans. I guess I'd passed the test. At least this one.

I wonder how many thousands upon thousands of people down through the ages have experienced this with, of course, different symbols and metaphors? How many of them are alive right now and in our midst, but we just don't recognize them? I hope to meet them. We have much to talk about.

The Aftermath

This is why I came to the woods. This is why I moved apart. Dreamers need space and time.

Again I ask the reoccurring question: Did all this happen in my mind?

Of course it did. At least, that's where the memory and interpretation of it exists. But at the time it felt so real that I find myself fully believing it. All of it. Every bit of it.

I am too grounded and too much the intellectual researcher to be swayed by mere fantasy. My whole life stands as a testament to rationality. A dreamer? Sure! Mystic? Sometimes, on the occasional second Tuesday. Optimist? Not so much, but once in a while. Practical? Always!

And now this.

To all my life's journeys, adventures, successes, and failures, to all that I have learned, sometimes at great cost, to all of my accumulated experiences, I can now add this: I have come to believe that the cosmos, this eternally mysterious and infinitely diverse place, has a plan for us. We were there when that plan was formed. Indeed, we probably even worked it out ourselves before we began this great adventure that we call life in this perception realm.

There are helpers and guides out there who care for us—who love us with the infinite love of Akasha itself. We are not alone. They are a part of our lives. We need only open our eyes and hearts to see their reality.

"Unseen angels," the Bible calls them in the book of Hebrews. The "Spirit Guides" of shamanic tradition. Our "Higher Self."

Someday we will meet them in a different realm, and oh, what a story we will have to tell!

FOUR
ENCOUNTERING THE BIZARRE:
A COSMIC THEORY

*"I found myself in a very strange place that I had never seen before ...
To one side, absorbed in the motions of a dance, I could see a giant figure
dressed in flowing white robes with black vertical markings."*
Graham Hancock in *Supernatural*

What's behind the Curtain?

August 27, 2012

After about an hour of meditation, in which my shortcomings were all
paraded before the perception of my mind, I had one, brief, terrible,
wonderful vision. I felt myself inside a great vortex of swirling energy. I
thought I had been at peace, but then it occurred to me that my mind was
in constant motion, trying to shape my experience and keep myself in the
vision. For an instant I was able to let go and surrender completely to what
was happening. My mind cut loose and drifted off into the void, and I was
suddenly aware of the whole universe being inside of me. I had expanded,
somehow. I could see planet Earth, hanging in space and surrounded by
stars, and I was the Cosmos. I didn't just experience it. I was the whole
universe. I engulfed it. I wasn't just looking at it. It existed within my body. For
a moment, I felt like God. Not "one with God." I was God, and the universe
was my creation.

As I write these words, this OBE happened to me more than five years ago. But
it is just as vivid now as it was then. I've thought about it often and it always
makes me wonder what happened, and whether or not what I saw and felt in

those brief moments at all resembled how things really are out there beyond our perception realm.

Is there a reality that exists beyond the sensory boundaries of our normal experience of life? Is there a Source from whence we originate, and to which we return? If so, can we access it on this side of physical death?

Obviously our scientific technology can't penetrate it. The many technological wonders that make up the toolkit of today's physicists, astronomers, and lab technicians were all invented to study things that exist within the confines of the material world. How can we study things that happen outside the world of atomic particles, out there on the other side of the Higgs Field? How do we put such things in a test tube or run them through a particle accelerator?

Maybe a familiar example will help bring the problem into focus.

The Technology of the Prism

Our eyes have evolved to identify things that reflect light. In the dead of night we are blind.

But what is light?

Right away we run into a problem. Less than a hundred years ago scientists discovered that we don't know the answer to that question. If we capture a beam of light in order to look closely at its composition or its position in space, we learn that light is a stream of particles traveling at 186,000 miles (299,000 kilometers) per second. But if we let it alone to do its thing, in its own way, we discover that light is a wave of energy. One way concludes that light consists of particles. The other determines that light consists of waves. Which is it?

The answer is—both! Not one or the other. Both at the same time. And whichever identity it assumes is not dependent upon some inherent quality it possesses, but rather the method you employ to describe it. *You* determine the very makeup of that which you seek to define. You, yourself, by your very act of observation, bring about the physical answer for which you seek.

Not very scientific, huh?

Let's go even further.

The light we see around us is actually a very narrow band of vibrational wavelengths. If we pass light through a simple piece of technology—a prism— we discover it breaks down into seven wavelengths called colors. Red, orange, yellow, green, blue, indigo, and violet. These colors comprise what we call the visible light spectrum. Each of these colors is a separate vibrational unity. They exist on totally different frequencies and are distinct from one another. But together they form a single entity that we call visible light.

Okay, fine! By using a piece of technology, a device known as a prism, we've discovered that light is composed of seven different frequencies of energy. End of story! Right?

Wrong!

Using more sophisticated technology we have determined that the visible light our eyes have evolved to see is only a very narrow band of the totality of the entire spectrum. Vibrating above our range of sight are previously unknown, but still practical and usable, light waves. Because we believed in them, rather than dismissing them as unreal because we couldn't see them, we've been able to study them and develop, for example, infrared devices to extend our range of sight even in the dark. We've learned to capture and utilize heat waves. We've invented radar guns and converted television frequencies into pixels which, when projected on a screen, seem to come alive with a life of their own. We've harnessed short-wave radio waves, broadcast frequencies and even longer radio waves.

On the other end of the scale we've learned that we have to protect ourselves from ultraviolet waves and X-rays, gamma rays and cosmic waves of unknown origin and frequencies that might reach to infinity.

Every one of these exotic light waves is a relatively new discovery, even though we've noticed their results, in some cases, for millions of years, ever since one of our distant ancestors developed the first case of sunburn. In other words, these non-visible light waves didn't just show up. They've been around since the Big Bang. But in my generation we first discovered and named them, and then invented ways to use them. Microwaves have been around for billions of years. They're not new. But recently we've used them to make lots of popcorn in microwave ovens. We finally caught on and harnessed their energy, that's all.

If you could sit down with your great-great-grandmother and describe an appliance that currently resides in virtually every modern kitchen in the western world, a scientific breakthrough that allows you to harness microwaves that vibrate at a frequency far too fast for her to see, she would think you were describing something totally bizarre. It would be completely outside of her mental box and she would probably think you a little crazy, even if in an affectionate way. She would have no experience at all sufficient to enable her to understand what you are talking about.

You understand it, because you have a microwave oven in your kitchen and you use it all the time. You may not understand *how* it works, but you know *that* it works, because you have used it time and time again to warm up leftovers. You may not understand the physics of it, but you appreciate its reality.

People who have never seen one in operation, however, will think you're imagining things.

From Metaphor to Meaning

That scenario mimics precisely the conversation we are about to have. I am about to engage in a far-flung depiction of reality that exists on a totally different frequency than that of our narrow perception realm. I am going to make the claim that such a reality is just as real as the microwaves that exist beyond our ability to see. I am further going to claim that such a reality is as perfectly natural as are light waves that vibrate outside our visual spectrum. The problem is that it exists beyond the experience of those people who aren't in the habit of looking for it. I'm going to try to describe that reality even though the words I will be forced to use are insufficient because they were invented to describe the familiar sights and sounds of *our* perception realm. I'm also going to claim that life at these frequencies can be experienced, just as ultraviolet light can give you a sunburn even though you don't see it.

What we're about to do together, in other words, is consider the fact that reality might exist on levels we don't usually observe. We're going to name it and claim it and try to make it just as practical as the Geiger Counters we use to indicate the presence of undetected radiation waves.

If you haven't experienced this reality, or if you have found it by accident and want to learn more about it, what's your reaction probably going to be? My guess is that you'll use the same word our hypothetical great-great-grandmother might have used if she encountered a microwave oven—bizarre!

Just as in the case of my microwave oven, I don't know *how* things work in this reality. But I know that it is real. I've seen it. And because it exists outside the normal activity that language was invented to describe, it seems, yes, bizarre. While you are in the moment it may seem normal. After all, reality is, well, real, even if it exists outside the boundaries of what you know. The problem comes when you come back under the influence of your normal senses and your brain is forced to file through your experiential vocabulary in order to come up with images and words to describe it all. That's when it starts to sound a bit bizarre.

Take these entries from my journal, for instance:

September 23, 2012

I feel myself going out of body, but somehow haven't quite prepared for it. Suddenly I find myself down at our Medicine Wheel, surrounded by a great, grey dome that cuts me off from the rest of the world. I ask what I need to learn here. (Kind of a prayer, "To whom it may concern.")

Immediately I am surrounded by ancient ones, perhaps American Indians, drumming and dancing in a circle around me. It's a good dance and I'm not concerned. It feels very real and somehow uplifting.

Then my physical nose starts to itch. I'm upset because I'm afraid that if I move my hand to scratch the itch, I will break the mood with physical movement. So I resist the urge.

The itch becomes intense and a funny thought occurs to me. I decide to treat this as if I am participating in a Sundance ritual. (In this ritual, an Indian seeking spiritual strength endures the agony of being pierced through his chest muscles with wooden rods and then hoisted by those rods up on a pole while other Indians dance around him, praying for him, while he seeks a vision. I could go on, but this is for the benefit of any who are not familiar with the Sundance. It's quite a spiritual exercise!)

I got quite a kick out of equating my itch with the pain of the Sundance. I thought it quite funny. One is so trivial and the other so intense. But the urge to scratch soon became unbelievable. It was all I could do to keep my hand still. Every time I thought it would subside, it came back worse than before. But I endured to the end, with one part of me fighting a great battle against caving in to the physical urge to scratch an itch and the other part laughing at the absurdity of a guy who sees any importance at all in such a trivial exercise.

I'm glad to announce, however, that my Sundance was a success. I resisted the urge to scratch and defeated all local principalities and powers. (Power to the people! We shall overcome!) And I returned to my body quite satisfied with myself, in spite of feeling a bit foolish.

I immediately decided to write this long night up in my journal. When I was about halfway finished, Barb got up to ask if I wanted to do a hot tub this morning. But as soon as she saw me sitting at the computer, she became quite concerned.

"What's wrong?" I asked.

"What did you do to your nose?" she answered. "It's covered in blood!"

Indeed it was. There was a scratch on the outside and it had bled quite a bit. By now it was dried up, but there it was. My nose was covered with crusted blood.

I went to check my pillow. I thought that maybe I had scratched myself in the night somehow. But there was nothing there. Apparently it had happened some time ago, though, because the blood was dried and had clotted. And I don't remember bumping into anything since I got up to meditate.

The part that caused the scratching temptation during my "Sundance" was on the right side. The scratch was on the left. I guess I must have bumped against something without knowing it ... right?

Now, what do you do with something like this? It lacks any objective evidence. It even, truth be told, sounds a bit silly.

But it happened, and seems somehow to have been important. So what does it mean?

I don't have the faintest idea. It's bizarre.

This next reflection is complicated. It happened over a period of years but somehow merged together into one bizarre experience. Earlier I shared some of this story. Edited for clarity, here's the rest of it:

October 2, 2014
Repair the tear - Become the door - Do it in love

Is there a "tear" in our space/time perception, through which we enter this realm? In today's vision I was stretched out like a thin plate or membrane—all the colors of the rainbow. I became the gate of my many dreams. I went to the Shaman's Circle and "held out" this gate, this door, for the shamans to walk through into a different realm—much like walking through a movie screen into a movie. I don't have the faintest idea what this means.

November 2, 2014

Since my last entry, I have been depressed and discouraged. It's hard to believe, but that's just the way it is. Perhaps the depression is a reaction. Perhaps it involves disappointment that things can't always be charged and exciting. Maybe I have to come to expect this reaction. But I stopped meditating, for the most part, and nothing much happened the few times I did. (I even wrote to Bill Buhlman about it and he wrote back telling me the same thing happened to him sometimes. He wrote a best-selling book about OBEs and teaches the subject all over the world. It's good to know that even the experts can have dry periods.) It has been a rough time.

Then, last night, or rather early this morning, everything explained itself. I simply can't find words to describe what happened. I now understand what was said of the Buddha at the time of his enlightenment. Buddhists claim that as he sat under the Bodhi Tree, the tree of enlightenment, he saw, in a moment of time, all his previous incarnations and understood the law of Karma at work, bringing him to this point.

That's what happened to me. It occurred at the time we change the clocks back—a significant symbolism. It even happened at the precise time we change them—1:00 AM. As best as I can find words, here's what happened:

I have had, so far, a very uncomfortable night. I just can't sleep except for a brief doze for a few minutes at a time. A few minutes before 1:00 a.m., Barb and I talked for a while. It was comforting and I soon tried to sleep again.

What followed seemed to be a very troubling, very vivid, dream. I was transported into the future—into a very technological society in which every person had a function to fulfill. It was a wild vision of pipes and tubes and scaffolding structure. I was trying, with a few others, to get out, but was thwarted at every turn. Our escape involved climbing and jumping from one structure to another, but we kept getting enmeshed and were barely able to proceed. Every move took us farther in and I felt panicked and very afraid. It was as if I was working my way into a three-dimensional maze that just kept getting more and more involved and convoluted.

Then something happened. I don't know how, but I came to the conclusion that I could fight back. My impression was that someone told me so, and maybe even began to lead the charge out. But we fought ourselves back through the maze, reversing our direction. I yelled something to the others. I remember it being something like, FREEDOM.

Barb says I did yell in my dream. But I said "Radio! What happened to the radio?" This makes sense. I once wrote a piece about dowsing entitled Turn Your Radio On. *It was about how our brains are receptors, rather than creators, of consciousness. The only way out of the maze/dream was to "tune into" outside help. Maybe…*

At any rate, we made it out. It was just like playing a movie in reverse. I became aware that we were gaining in our escape because we were going over the same ground that trapped us, but in reverse. I was undoing the past. As we approached the perimeter of the structure/maze/scaffolding, a bus was waiting for us. Now things really began to move quickly! The bus was there to carry us back to where we began. There were seven exits that led to my destination—the place from which I had started. But the bus was moving so quickly I had to jump fast. I barely made the seventh exit, but it was enough. I arrived back at my destination and suddenly woke up, feeling grateful that it was just a dream.

But it doesn't stop there.

As soon as I was awake I was very conscious of the fact that I was out of body. The scenes kept rolling back in time. I was fully alert and conscious that the two hemispheres of my brain were working independently. My intuitive side (right brain) was reeling back the past lives. My analytical side (left brain) was critically scrutinizing the process. They were both completely functional and fully alert.

On the one hand, I saw in a flash, hundreds, perhaps thousands, of past lives go by and felt fully familiar with every one of them. I was aware of every choice I had ever made. I understood exactly why things have played out as they have. I was following the course of Karma that led to the horrible future world I had just encountered. I went all the way back to the beginning—much too much to possibly recall and write down. But I was fully aware and reasoning, faster than the speed of light. I saw how the past led inevitably to the future.

Then the movie suddenly stopped. I was aware of being on this spot of ground, the property where we now live, thousands of years ago. It was the time Barb, in a previous incarnation, had discovered Earth Energy here at this place.

Here's how I wrote about it back in 2012:

August 26, 2012

Although I don't feel any movement I am conscious of the fact that my body is in the chair but I am standing up, talking to Sobuko, my spirit guide. I make an affirmation that I want to experience this land as it was when Barb and I were here together, a long time ago. The image I have of our land changes. The trees are gone. Instead, I see a hillside covered with thin soil, brown grass, about knee high, if that, and lots and lots of rocks. I even seem to remember something about mammoths grazing in the distance. There is a "tribe" of people around us, although tribe is not a good word. A big family is more like it. I'm not really conscious of anyone except Barb. She is here. She's not much different in size than she is now, and I'm aware that I "inhabit" her body as well. But I'm only her "male" side, so to speak. She is predominate—she's in charge.

She has just "discovered," for lack of a better word, the earth energy here on this spot of ground. This is totally new to her and to her people, and she has no language for it. She only knows that something about a certain spot of ground, right where our Medicine Wheel now stands, intrigues her. She makes a small pile of stones right where the center of our Medicine Wheel now is. She walks the pathway that now connects to our spiral. She discovers the place where the energy seems to meet near the middle. All these places she marks with small piles of rocks. She has discovered something but doesn't know exactly what.

She tries to enlist the help of some of her people, but they aren't really interested. They harbor no bad feelings. They just don't see the importance of it. They have better things to do. They're busy! This is a rock quarry where they come every year or two to get the material they need to make tools for the coming season. What good does it do to pile rocks up and think about them in any way other than natural resources?

They humor her. But that's about it.

Near the end of their stay here, something happens. A flood sweeps over Barb's rock piles, completely destroying them. It's not a great tragedy. Floods happen all the time. And, after all, Barb built her stone piles right at a place floods sometimes happen anyway. What did she expect?

But Barb is still intrigued. She wants to come back and explore this idea some more. Without making a big metaphysical deal out of the whole thing, she finds a rock that is shaped somewhat like the hawks which are beginning their migration patterns and filling the sky with their shrill "kreeees." Hawks have always had a special meaning for her. With a few hits, taps, and strikes she quickly shapes the rough form of a hawk from the stone she holds in her hands. She places it in a safe place, uphill from the flood, and vows to return to take up her quest of discovery—her interest in Earth Energy—here at this spot of ground.

And she finally does return—thousands of years later.

Now the story changes. An alternative version begins. Instead of not finding anyone to listen, she finds one person who cares and comforts her. It's me! I step out of the crowd, embrace her and reinforce her discovery. This time, I realize she was so discouraged she was going to throw the hawk away, in disappointment. But because I was there and believed her, she hid the hawk instead of throwing it away.

That's the reason we now have it, and it became the moment that bound us forever. While embracing her in that moment I noticed something on the ground. All I can say is that it looked like a French Fry. It wasn't, of course. They wouldn't be invented for thousands of years. But I picked it up and moved it, knowing, even while I did it, that I was somehow changing history. It was the Butterfly Effect—a small change at a precise moment that altered the course of everything to follow.

Suddenly I knew what I had done. I had gone back in time and "repaired the tear" (See October 2 above). In that past, or probably alternate, life, I had let Barb go it alone. I had "torn" our relationship. The alternate future that I had dreamed about, a technological maze and trap, would have been our lot. We would have faced our future separate and alone. But because I had gone back in time and changed a single moment, the moment of the discovery of Earth Energy here on this spot of land, I had changed the future. That moment led to countless lives together, working on Earth Energy, and culminated in the one we now lead, our final life on earth in this perception reality. We have come full circle, with hawk showing the way. I have "become the door" leading to this moment in time instead of the alternatives. Out of the thousands of realities that might have happened, this one became possible. And it was made possible through love.

Repair the tear - Become the door - Do it in love

Now it all makes sense. There is so much more, but it is becoming harder and harder to capture it with the futility of words as time passes. It seems to be the most powerful spiritual experience of my life. Love seems to be flowing out to the world. The tear has been repaired.

It has been a humbling morning!

Time Out

Before we can continue I need your understanding about something important. Revisiting these entries from my journal has caused some confusion in my mind, and no doubt yours as well. I entered this account into my journal on November 2, 2014. But in doing so I had to thumb back the pages to an August 26, 2012 entry. Now that I commit them to book form, however, I'm reminded that what I call a Dream/Vision from August 12, 2012 seems to contradict, or at least muddy the waters, of the whole hawk effigy link. The vision of August 12th came in the form of a full blown story. Two weeks later, on August 26th, the OBE involved different concepts involving time and past lives. I don't know how to handle the discrepancies.

I must admit that the writer in me is tempted to rewrite both versions, bringing them into some kind of harmony. It would be easy to do, and without access to my dream journal you'd never know the difference.

But I'm using my journal entries as arguments that OBEs are real. If I start changing them around I'd be tampering with evidence. That would be dishonest and I can't live with that. So we're stuck with a real quandary that, as I see it, has only a few explanations.

1. I wrote the two entries as soon as I could following the actual experiences. But I might have remembered them differently than they actually occurred. Even an explanation of a normal dream sometimes changes in the telling without any attempt of deception on the part of the dreamer. Our brains tend to try to fill in the gaps of the narrative, so to speak. It happens. That's why police try to interview witnesses of an accident as soon as possible after the accident occurs. The more time passes, the more the stories differ.

2. Given the emphasis on time in the second entry, I could very well have witnessed two differing versions of the same incident played out in two parallel time periods, each stemming from a past consistent with the actions of that particular period. I'll have more to say about this later on. It's called the *Many Worlds Hypothesis*.

3. It could very well be that I witnessed two completely different incidents that happened at least a few hundred, maybe even a few thousand years apart. The hawk effigy would then be the common thread linking the two scenarios which implies the reality of past life regression. If you count our discovering it in our current lifetime, it links three such lives together. (In case this proves to be true, Barb and I have now made arrangements so that before our passing we're going to return the effigy to the woods. Who knows? Maybe a future time traveler will discover it once again in a few hundred years!)

Any one of these explanations may prove to be correct. I just don't know right now. Maybe someday I will. I hope so!

Order out of Bizarre Chaos

What does all this mean? I'm about to attempt some kind of explanation. But in doing so I will also try to arrive at a theory of OBE travel involving what I call the Quantum Akashic Field. In doing so we'll follow the steps of what is known as the scientific method:

- We've discovered a phenomenon that we wish to explore—namely, the Out-of-Body Experience.
- So far we've been gathering evidence of its existence.
- In this chapter we'll formulate a hypothesis.
- In the next chapter we'll consider three lines of evidence.
- Then, in Part Two, we'll move on to experimentation.

- Finally, we'll sum up the whole argument and publish it in this book for peer review.

Step by step then, here we go.

I've shared some of my own Out-of-Body Experiences. There are undoubtedly those of you who are now trying to explain away those experiences as being psychological in nature—perhaps self-hypnosis, an active dream life, flights of imagination, or even the self-centered, ego-based, whimsical musings of someone who has lived alone in the woods for too long and could use a healthy dose of reality.

Believe me, if you harbor those doubts, I don't blame you a bit. During the bulk of my time on earth over the last 70 years I would have had them as well.

But I now doubt the doubts. I think I've discovered something real. There are compelling reasons for deducing the presence of the Quantum Akashic Field and our ability to perceive it during Out-of-Body Experiences. I've come to believe that this field supports not only life as we know it, but what to us seems like a bizarre life we haven't even fully encountered yet, and probably will never really understand until we leave this physical realm via the process we call death. We'll consider the three lines of evidence I've uncovered in the next chapter. But for now, let's try to develop a simple-to-understand hypothesis so we'll have a goal to shoot for.

A Quantum Akashic Field Hypothesis

What is the *Quantum Akashic Field?*

Here's how I have come to understand it. I certainly don't think this is a perfect definition. My own opinions will undoubtedly change and evolve as I learn more. But it's a place to start.

Everything in all of creation is connected, or entangled, through what I have variously called energy lines, vortexes, spirals, and grids. I've come to believe that all of us can consciously experience that connection through a process of Out-of-Body Experiences, using a form of what I like to call quantum intuition. We are all supported by a universal field, an "information" field that Carl Jung labeled the Collective Unconscious and Ervin Laszlo dubbed the Akashic Field.

It is a power field, the ground of our being—a mystical grid that is at the same time both magical and real.

Einstein accessed it. What do you think he was doing when he engaged in his famous thought experiments? So did Newton, Socrates, Beethoven, Brahms, Mozart, the builders of ancient monuments, ancient dowsers, Hindu mystics, and every other genius who ever lived. The reason people built similar pyramids in Egypt, Asia, Central America, and Peru was that they were accessing the same information field. The reason societies started doing the same things with stone at the same time was because they were all tuned in to the same source. When it appeared in Akasha, everyone, everywhere, had access to it.

Each of us is a physically manifested expression of an energetic possibility that originated in Akasha.

The ancients hadn't understood the science of all this. They just sensed that they were in the presence of something bigger than themselves. They felt its energy coursing through them like blood through an artery.

We, living in this modern world, have buried those feelings under years and years of cultural debitage. But sometimes, when conditions are right, they rise to the surface in dreams, visions and Out-of-Body Experiences. Then we realize we are part of a mystery that is much bigger than ourselves. In those moments we move outside our sensory filters and perceive something larger than life as we know it.

Does the world of Faery exist? Are leprechauns and gnomes more than mythic representations of subdued human traits? Do worlds exist wherein half-animal, half-human entities roam?

Absolutely! Akasha is a field of infinite potentiality. If you can imagine it, it exists somewhere. As a matter of fact, the very act of imagining it brings it into existence. The world around us, the familiar world of house and home, of communities and wilderness, of death and taxes, is a product of deliberate intention. We are living in a dream-world of cosmic thought, designed to produce and teach the Great Illusion of individuality and separateness. How else could we possibly ever have experienced such a thing if we didn't intentionally produce it ourselves by "imagining" it into existence?

Please understand this. It's extremely important. Your senses rebel against the very idea of ours being only one of an infinite, impossibly extravagant number of worlds, but, as we shall see when we examine the evidence in the next chapter, this is not the New Age musing of an out-of-touch mystic. There are good reasons to deduce that everything we can imagine exists somewhere out there in the Multiverse.

We're talking about infinity, here. We're talking about eternity. Infinity isn't just a great big space. Eternity isn't just a long, long time. Infinity has nothing to do with space. It has no boundaries. Eternity isn't a long, long time. It has nothing to do with time. There is plenty of "space" and plenty of "time" to produce absolutely anything and everything. As a matter of fact, that may be the whole point of creation—to produce the experience of absolutely everything.

When you "travel" out of body, that's what you're observing. You journey to different landscapes and encounter different suburbs of reality. It's not imagination. It's real. It may seem esoteric and bizarre. But *our* world undoubtedly seems bizarre to the entities that inhabit the landscapes which you encounter out there. Life takes myriad forms. In the depths of the ocean, for instance, you can encounter truly bizarre life forms. They probably think you're pretty bizarre, too.

So out-of-body travel isn't necessarily exotic. It just seems that way. Think of being transported to a totally different country with totally different architecture and people who practice totally different customs—and multiply it by a million or so. Then you've got it.

The Quantum Akashic Field is a field of infinite possibilities, each of which is realized somewhere, somehow, sometime. We live in one of them. It feels as though ours is unique and alone because under normal conditions it's the only one available for us to experience with our five senses.

But OBEs are not normal. They are *extra*-sensory. That's all there is to it. Simple, huh?

A Metaphor for the Journey

Maybe it's time for a good metaphor. Earlier I said we can never say, "This is the way it is." The best we can do is say, "This is what it looked like to me." This is how I often describe it when I give talks such as my YouTube presentation on *Quantum Dowsing*. (You can access it through my website, *www.jimwillis.net*, or directly at *www.youtube.com/watch?v=NwXlNhvHls8*.)

We'll begin at what I call the *Source*. Use whatever word works for you. Call it God. Call it All That Is, the Ultimate Mystery, or even Great Spirit. Call it whatever name resonates with you. It's the still point at the center of the circle of life. It's the beginning and end of all that is. As we continue, I'll just call it the Source.

What is it? No one knows. Where is it? Everywhere. And nowhere. No one can even really imagine it. But picture it in your mind as best you can, even if it is just a total mystery at this point.

Now picture yourself as a wave of some kind of energy within that Source. You have no shape or form. You take up no space but contain infinite possibility. You travel at no speed and exist in perfect rest, but have infinite potential.

With you in the Source there are an infinite number of other waves, but that fact isn't really apparent because all waves are One Wave. You certainly can't say there exists anything approaching individuality, because all is One. But you cannot grow and personally develop through such one-ness. The only way to do so is to develop uniqueness. And the only way to do that is through individual experience.

And so it begins. A single wave breaks out, beginning its journey toward uniqueness, toward individuality, towards singular experience. When every wave in the Source undergoes such transformation, each on its own journey, total potentiality becomes possible. All it requires is a space and time for every single possible experience to become realized. When all such waves finally unite back home, the Source will then have become, through you and every other wave that experienced uniqueness, everything. Every possible potentiality will have been realized. The Source will have become infinitely realized possibility.

There are, of course, problems inherent to this process. *Realized* possibilities are not always *nice* possibilities. To put it simply, potentiality has a downside. We call it good and bad. The Chinese say it is yin and yang. Buddhists prefer the phrase, "pairs of opposites." In short, duality enters the picture.

When you begin a journey out from the Source, out *from* Unity and *toward* individuality, you begin the process of establishing your "Self," which, by definition, is separate from Unity. The whole process of evolution is a mechanism through which we move from *innocent* unity through an agonizing experience of separation and heartache, to the point where we return to *mature* unity accompanied by individual experience and development.

Now let's think about the journey out from the Source which each one of us has begun. Picture again that wave of potential that will become you. Your journey begins. You move out from the Source. Where do you first find yourself? What environment do you now inhabit?

I like to use the word *Consciousness*. It is what both Albert Einstein and Stephen Hawking once called "The Mind of God."

Although you still have no mass, either physical or metaphysical, you are now what I might describe as being a little thicker or heavier. You haven't yet visualized where you are going or what you will look like, but you are aware that eventually you will.

The "Mind of God" is an interesting place. There is still complete unity, but there is also a heightened awareness that something we can only call uniqueness and individuality exist. What's it like to be different from every other wave? What does it feel like to be alone, for instance? How will you react to an experience no other wave has ever known? It's a temptation, isn't it?

There's only one way to find out. You have to travel onward. You sample the "forbidden fruit" of "the knowledge of good and evil," of duality, and discover that rather than being a sin, it is an important step in your development. It's time to leave Eden.

The First Step of the Journey

Your journey now takes you through your first defining field. It's a place wherein you begin to take on shape. Not mass. Not yet. But you grow a little heavier as you begin to transform yourself into something truly unique and separate.

Taking a cue from the ancient Hindus, I call this place of transformation the *Akashic Field.* Everything that we know and experience around us, every rock, tree, and flower, every person, animal, bird, and fish, and every landscape we discover as we travel out of body, was first conceived in *Akasha.*

You have now gathered what we might call "metaphysical" mass. You understand the concept of individuality. By that I mean that you understand how unique individuality leads to unique experience. You pass through the Akashic Field and become something different. You now have some direction. When you emerge from the Akashic Field you find yourself in a totally different realm. You have now entered *Quantum Reality.* This world was discovered by our scientists only about a hundred years ago. We are just now beginning to explore it.

Sir James Hopwood Jeans, a brilliant English physicist, astronomer, and mathematician, once said that "the universe (now) begins to look more like a great *thought* than a great *machine.*" For this reason I call the world of quantum reality the place of *thoughts* and *intentions.*

Now, please understand. You're not human yet. You still have a way to go. But here in this world you can now form what might be called a *thought* about what a human is, and form an *intention* that you're going to be one.

Quantum reality is thus a place of potential. Humans don't really live here. Not yet, anyway. The *potential* for any one human is here. That potential will soon be realized when it comes time to take one more step. In order for a human to develop, the thought must first collapse into the environment humans experience. To do that it must pass through the newly discovered *Higgs Field.*

The Second Step of the Journey

The Higgs Field is a mysterious, proven reality, but it's very difficult to describe. Named after Peter Higgs, who predicted its existence purely through mathematical computations, most theoretical physicists believe it to be an energy field that exists everywhere, permeating the realm of the reality we perceive.

On our side of the Higgs field the laws of physics begin to apply. It's most often described as being something like molasses, through which energy flows from "somewhere" to here. The field slows down the energy particles, bulking them up and giving them mass, because they no longer travel at a speed sufficient to retain their original identity. The "E" (Energy) of Einstein's famous equation ($E=mc^2$) no longer maintains its infinite and immediate velocity. It becomes denser. In other words, energy collapses into the mass we call matter, the substance that is perceived by our senses. In order to convert mass back into energy it needs to attain not just the speed of light, but the speed of light squared. Were it not for the Higgs Field, particles would not have enough mass to attract each other by means of the law of gravity. They would not clump together to form what we call objects. They would just float around in an energetic state, oblivious to one another.

It's important to remember that the Higgs Field doesn't *generate* mass. It doesn't *create* the particles. That would be impossible, given the accepted laws of conservation of energy. All it does is slow energy down so the laws of physics controlling our side of the field can take over and work their magic— the magic called the *Higgs Effect*. Particles-in-being that pass through the Higgs Field gain mass because they slow down, clump together through gravitational force, and form measurable objects.

Does that help? Don't worry if the details leave you dizzy. Just stick to the main idea.

We have now arrived at the familiar world of our five senses. We're in the familiar material realm of trees and flowers, our next-door neighbors and, more importantly, scientists, who can now breathe a lot easier because they have something to measure and put under a microscope. It's the world we see around us.

But even this world has its hidden realms. I'm referring to the Cosmos in all its many manifestations. Here lies the *Multiverse* in its infinite capacity for creativity. Here dwell all possible manifestations of every single possibility. Here lie an infinite number of "yous," each living their own life in woeful ignorance of their doppelgangers in parallel universes. These are the bizarre worlds we experience when we travel out of body.

They all seem to be supported by unseen energy, call it a form of *Dark Matter*, that pushes everything out towards infinity. This is where we find the mysteries inherent in the mathematics of theoretical physics. This is the home of String Theory, Membrane Theory, and all the other fantastic ideas circulating around great academic institutions, eventually spilling out to TV shows on the Discovery Channel. This is what intrigues and mystifies people today.

Journey Home

We began this whole journey, you'll remember, back at the Source. There we started out with a vague notion of individual expression encased within perfect Unity. Out here, on the edge, every one of those expressions is manifested. Infinite being. Eternal experiment. Countless worlds. Each different and unique.

And sometimes they overlap just a bit. Every world we visit while out of body exists for the same reason. They are theaters wherein the actors, us, and countless other sentient beings, can all experience uniqueness, something impossible to achieve in the place of total unity.

Our senses have evolved to enable us to experience life in *this* perception realm. But that doesn't mean others are not available to us. That's what Out-of-Body Experience is all about. We by-pass our senses and experience something outside our perceptions. We travel to new worlds. We journey outward.

In doing so we experience myriad opportunities. Perhaps we even visit places we might want to inhabit for a while some day when our life span here has reached its end. Who knows?

Is there any proof that the reality I just described actually exists? Am I even close to describing the truth of our existence?

I believe such evidence *does* actually exist. In the next chapter we're going to examine three distinct lines of such evidence. Stick with me! We're almost home!

Before we turn to the evidence, let's recap the theory once more:

The Quantum Akashic Field is a field of infinite possibilities, each of which is realized somewhere, somehow, sometime. We live in one of them. It feels as though ours is unique and alone because under normal conditions it's the only one available for us to experience with our five senses. But OBEs are *not* normal. They are *extra*-sensory. That's all there is to it.

FIVE
THREE LINES OF EVIDENCE

It is not only permissible to doubt the absolute validity of space-time perception;
it is, in view of the available facts, even imperative to do so.
Carl Jung in *Psychology of the Occult*

Searching for Answers

I've just made quite a substantial claim. If it's false, we can file it away under metaphysical nonsense—fun, but not to be taken seriously. If it's true, and serious people start to take it seriously, nothing will ever be the same again.

But serious claims require serious proof. And even if a world of reality exists outside our presumed ability to detect it, what good will it do to discover it? Does it offer us any practical help in our day-to-day life? Will it have any effect on us? Why should we even care? The answers to these questions are important.

Practical Help?

First of all, in terms of quantum reality offering us any practical help in our day to day lives, we have to respond with a firm, "maybe!"

It might turn out that the fields of medicine and psychology would greatly benefit from serious study of parallel worlds and contact between them. Those suffering from schizophrenia, for instance, often hear voices or report the presence of people who are invisible to others. Patients who exhibit multiple personalities can baffle therapists. Epilepsy has been called the "spiritual disease" ever since the time of Aristotle because a person experiencing a seizure often reports seeing other realities.

Are these people "sick?" Or are they actually interacting with parallel dimensions? Have specialists been too quick to simply prescribe medicine that shuts down the part of the brain that experiences such sights and sounds? Might we do better to examine such experiences with an open mind?

Our culture could very well benefit from such studies. Shamans and holy men have long been ridiculed as simple-minded victims of schizophrenic crack-ups. Their followers have often been described as deluded, superstition-prone primitives. Historically, cases of possession have often been attributed to epileptic seizures. Multiple personality disorders detected under hypnosis are usually dismissed as outright frauds. Maybe it's time to reassess our cultural bias.

Another reason to study NDEs and OBEs is that most people who experience them come back with a feeling of peace. Over and over again we hear that such people are no longer afraid of death. In a healthy way, many even come to embrace their ultimate demise. They look forward to it without any suicidal tendencies. In short, an OBE can bring about a healthy zest for life and ease the transition into death that we all must make someday.

Medical research into OBEs is one practical way in which it might be valuable to take the claims of parallel universes seriously. But what about actual proof?

It seems to me that there are at least three lines of evidence that point to a greater reality than that which we normally experience. Let's examine them one at a time.

ONE
Legends, Myths, Religious Texts, and Oral History

The first line of evidence is found in legends, myths, religious texts, and the rich oral history found all over the world. I covered this topic in great detail in my book, *Supernatural Gods*. There's far too much evidence to repeat it all here, so let's stick to a few well-known examples that permeate the major religious traditions practiced by a majority of people in western cultures. As these examples show, evidence for parallel dimensions has been hiding in plain sight for thousands of years.

Take this well-known excerpt from a much-read book in the Hebrew Scriptures. Christians and Muslims call them the Old Testament. It comes from the book of Ezekiel:

> "In my thirtieth year, in the fourth month on the fifth day, while I was among the exiles by the Kebar River, the heavens were opened and I saw visions of God...

I looked, and I saw a windstorm coming out of the north—an immense cloud with flashing lightning and surrounded by brilliant light. The center of the fire looked like glowing metal, and in the fire were what looked like four living creatures. In appearance their form was human, but each of them had four faces and four wings. Their legs were straight; their feet were like those of a calf and gleamed like burnished bronze. Under their wings on their four sides they had human hands. All four of them had faces and wings, and the wings of one touched the wings of another. Each one went straight ahead; they did not turn as they moved.

Their faces looked like this: Each of the four had the face of a human being, and on the right side each had the face of a lion, and on the left the face of an ox; each also had the face of an eagle. Such were their faces. They each had two wings spreading out upward, each wing touching that of the creature on either side; and each had two other wings covering its body. Each one went straight ahead. Wherever the spirit would go, they would go, without turning as they went. The appearance of the living creatures was like burning coals of fire or like torches. Fire moved back and forth among the creatures; it was bright, and lightning flashed out of it. The creatures sped back and forth like flashes of lightning.

As I looked at the living creatures, I saw a wheel on the ground beside each creature with its four faces. This was the appearance and structure of the wheels: They sparkled like topaz, and all four looked alike. Each appeared to be made like a wheel intersecting a wheel. As they moved, they would go in any one of the four directions the creatures faced; the wheels did not change direction as the creatures went. Their rims were high and awesome, and all four rims were full of eyes all around.

When the living creatures moved, the wheels beside them moved; and when the living creatures rose from the ground, the wheels also rose. Wherever the spirit would go, they would go, and the wheels would rise along with them, because the spirit of the living creatures was in the wheels. When the creatures moved, they also moved; when the creatures stood still, they also stood still; and when the creatures rose from the ground, the wheels rose along with them, because the spirit of the living creatures was in the wheels.

Spread out above the heads of the living creatures was what looked something like a vault, sparkling like crystal, and awesome. Under the vault their wings were stretched out one toward the other, and each had two wings covering its body. When the creatures moved, I heard the sound of their wings, like the roar of rushing waters, like the voice of the Almighty, like the tumult of an army. When they stood still, they lowered their wings.

Then there came a voice from above the vault over their heads as they stood with lowered wings. Above the vault over their heads was what looked like a throne of lapis lazuli, and high above on the throne was a figure like that of a man. I saw that from what appeared to be his waist up he looked like glowing metal, as if full of fire, and that from there down he looked like fire; and brilliant light surrounded him. Like the appearance of a rainbow in the clouds on a rainy day, so was the radiance around him.

This was the appearance of the likeness of the glory of the Lord. When I saw it, I fell facedown, and I heard the voice of one speaking.

He said to me, 'Son of Man, stand up on your feet and I will speak to you.'"

Ezekiel, chapter 1. New International Version of the Bible

When freed from its multi-millennial, religious, and cultural baggage, this appears to be the testimony of a respected Jewish prophet, a shaman, if you will, who reports an encounter with an entity from another dimension. It demonstrates all the classic hallmarks—otherworldly beings who are half-animal and half-human, an advanced technology completely foreign to modern understanding, and a message to bring back to the rest of the tribe.

Did Ezekiel just make up the whole thing? Was he mad? Or is this a faithful representation of something he actually experienced once he found himself free of the shackles of his normal five senses?

Ezekiel isn't alone. The Bible is full of such testimonies. Angels step out of the ether to sing hymns of joy, release an apostle from prison, or deliver important messages. Heavenly beings show up in times of need. The Apostle Paul himself, in II Corinthians, says he "traveled" to Heaven, "Whether in the body or out, I know not … God knows!"

Thus, anyone who takes the Bible seriously, but discounts parallel, inhabited dimensions as superstitions or flights of fancy, has some serious soul-searching to do. The two beliefs are logically inconsistent. The Bible is full of stories of parallel dimensions and travel between them—both ways.

And it's not just western, biblical religions that describe them. Here's an example, for instance, of a text found in the *Bhagavata Purana*, a sacred Hindu text that goes back more than 2,500 years:

"Every universe is covered by seven layers—earth, water, fire, air, sky, the total energy, and false ego. Each is ten times greater than the previous one. There are innumerable universes besides this one. Although they are unlimitedly large, they move about like points within you. Therefore you are unlimited."

Bhagavata Purana 6. 16. 37

Accounts such as these are universal, found in virtually every culture on earth. They go back as far as written language itself and, if oral history is to be believed, to the misty beginnings of humanity itself.

It would seem, then, that our very earliest ancestors were somehow in at least intuitive contact with counterparts from extra-sensory landscapes. Who knows? Perhaps in those mysterious dimensions we will someday find our own ancestral roots.

TWO
Eye Witness Testimonies

In any court proceeding, a good lawyer knows that the more corroborating witnesses he or she can produce, the better the case looks to a jury.

In the case of OBEs vs. Skeptics, there is no lack of such eye-witness testimony. Indeed, they are far too numerous to even begin to call them all to the stand. They number in the millions.

Here's a typical one, chosen at random from accounts compiled by Tara MacIsaac for the *Epoch Times* and posted on February 15, 2014:

"[My friend] claimed he was able to leave his body during sleep and basically travel around in his spirit form. I took it with a grain of salt for obvious reasons, but I didn't dismiss him right off the bat because I knew him pretty well and he wasn't the type of kid that would try to troll me about these things.

At the end of the night [of hanging out at my place], I told him, 'Hey, why don't you prove to me that you can really fly around as a spirit and come to my room tonight [traveling from his house to mine during sleep]?'

I came up with the idea that I would write a note on a post-it and he would have to guess what I wrote. He agreed.

Fast forward to the next morning. I get a call from him telling me that he had read the note. He got it right.

This experience has really blown my mind. I know it would be hard for most of you to believe me, but this really happened and I am 100 percent positive that there was no way he could have seen what I had written on that post-it."

Could this story, and perhaps many more like it, be fictitious? Of course! Could the writer have made up the whole thing? Sure. After all, there were no scientists trailing along, checking details. Could it consist of the results of a healthy imagination? Yes.

But there are so many of these kinds of stories that after reading through a hundred or so you can't help but wonder why so many people would try to deceive us about this. Can that many people be delusional, especially when the accounts share so many commonalities, are separated by so many cultural differences, and go back so far in time? There are simply too many eye-witnesses to ignore.

Sometimes a clever lawyer will go beyond random, eye-witness accounts and call to the stands a specialist—one who is an accredited professional. It's the duty of such a witness to provide clear, concise, unbiased, scientific evidence.

Let's now call such a witness to the stand. His name is Dean Radin, PhD, the Chief Scientist at the Institute of Noetic Science in California.

Dr. Radin originally trained as a concert violinist, but when you earn a degree in electrical engineering, *magna cum laude*, with honors in physics, and go on to eventually earn a PhD in psychology, it's hard to keep you down on the farm. (When I contacted him once with questions concerning one of his books, I mentioned that we shared an interest in bluegrass music. He assured me that though he was rusty, in his mind, "he could still play like the wind!")

On his website he is careful to note that he is not a psychic. He "is a scientist who conducts research on psychic phenomena," and has pursued "the far reaches of human consciousness, principally psi phenomena, using the tools of science," for the bulk of his career.

(Note: *Psi Phenomena* refers to what is often called "parapsychology" functions of the mind, such as extrasensory perception, precognition, and psychokinesis.)

Let's let him explain his interests in his own words, quoting from his website:

"Understanding this realm of human experience thus offers more than mere academic interest—it touches upon the very best that the human intellect and spirit have had to offer ... I am comfortable tolerating the ambiguity of not knowing the 'right answer,' which is a constant companion at the frontier."

My purpose in quoting him here is not to explain his findings. He does that himself in books listed in the Further Reading section at the end of this book. I expect he would take with a grain of salt, to put it mildly, some of the experiences I have described within these pages.

But his work at the Noetic Institute is an excellent example of scrutinized, peer-reviewed studies that are undertaken today—work that is often disparaged by traditional sources—pointing to the fact that if we are going to take reality seriously, we need to expand our parochial prejudices and open our minds about the subject.

As Dr. Radin puts it so well:

> "There is a huge anecdotal literature about psychic phenomena, but the evidence that convinced me is not only the results of my own experimental studies, but analysis of the cumulative, empirical evidence collected by qualified scientists under well-controlled conditions, and published in peer-reviewed scientific journals."
>
> **www.deanradin.org**

In short, OBE research and parapsychology studies, in which people are tested under controlled conditions, *is* underway. We just don't hear very much about it. Maybe the time has come for that to change. If so, the impetus will probably have to begin in the court of public opinion.

Indeed, because of some entertaining and informative TV shows, that movement has already started. There are plenty of witnesses. Together, they form a mighty chorus indeed. They have been in our midst for thousands of years. Their voices are often drowned out in the press of public affairs. To complicate things, even a quick Internet search reveals that quacks and charlatans are legion in this field. But modern editors, some scientists, many researchers, and countless participants are doing a good job weeding them out. The future begins to brighten a bit.

THREE
Theories of Science

This leads us to our final line of evidence. Is there a scientific basis for believing that the Quantum Akashic Field, astral travel, and parallel worlds inhabited by intelligent entities actually exist? Can we accept Out-of-Body Experiences and still maintain our intelligence? Is there a place at the table in this modern, educated, and sophisticated world for those who are curious and attracted to what we have been discussing so far?

In a word—yes! A century ago such a thing would have been unthinkable. Metaphysical reality had to be accepted on faith and circumstantial evidence. It was the stuff of religions, myths, and superstition. The physics of that day said there was simply no way to peer into such subjects, so it was forbidden to speculate about them in academic circles. Back in the 1970s and 80s, symposiums held to study the origins of the universe often insisted at the outset that any mention of God was taboo. "Believers" were legion, to be sure, but were, in many cases, patronized by the scientific community, if not subjected to outright scorn.

Then came early public familiarity with the quantum world, and things have never been the same. Quantum theory not only left room for such speculation—it demanded it.

In order to place that last sentence in context we're going to have to study the difference between classical and quantum physics. If you're not used to swimming in these oceans, you can develop the bends if you're not careful. But don't worry. I'm not going to go into depths that are over your head. I promise! No mathematical formulas. The concepts we'll discuss will keep us close to shore. But if we're going to talk about the scientific sea-change that has occurred over the last hundred years we have to test the waters and eventually jump in.

Here goes!

Classical Physics

Classical physics is often called *Newtonian* physics because its basis and mathematical formulas were first brought together in a systematic way by Isaac Newton. This system of thought is now so prevalent that folks should be excused if they think it's the only way to view the world. It describes the logical way things work in the visible world around us.

It's governed by laws and rules. Step off a cliff and you'll fall victim to the law of gravity. Play a game of billiards and you'll soon become familiar with rules governing action and reaction. Live long enough and you'll discover the principles of entropy every morning when you try to get out of bed.

Newton didn't invent these laws. He just developed the standard mathematical formulas used to describe them. People were using classical physics long before old Isaac came along.

Consider soldiers who shot cannons, for instance. It was common practice to "sight in" ordnance by firing a test shot and watching to see where the cannonball hit. If it landed twenty feet short and ten feet to the right of the target, a good gunner would elevate the barrel to correct for the pull of gravity and adjust a little to the left. He didn't compute for trajectory and windage. He just did what intuitively seemed correct ever since the first Neanderthal threw the first spear at a mastodon.

Newton didn't change any of this. The laws were perfectly understood and practical when used out in the field. What he did was bring them into the realm of academic and systematic scientific inquiry. He deduced, for instance, the mathematical formulation for a parabola—the path traced by a cannonball. If you knew all the variables, such as the pull of gravity on a certain size cannonball of a specific weight, the amount of force generated by a finite number of grains of gunpowder, the resistance encountered due to climatic conditions, and all the rest, you could, using mathematics alone, accurately predict where the cannonball would strike. If you wanted to adjust the impact area, all you had to do was change one or more of the variables. Adjust the amount of gunpowder, elevate the barrel, or account for wind gusts, and you were ready to wreak havoc upon the enemy.

You do much the same thing when you water your lawn. The water coming through your hose traces a parabola through the air. If you want to reach that far-away section of turf, you raise the hose and restrict the flow of water with your thumb, forcing the same amount of liquid to flow through a smaller opening, increasing its pressure and, therefore, its speed. The result is that you gain enough yardage to deliver your payload a bit farther than before. It's all about mathematics, whether you think of it in those terms or not.

In classical physics there are rules. We learn to follow them, whether we understand them or not, because they work. It's common sense.

Quantum/Physics *world*

Then came the discovery of the quantum world—the world of the very small. Low and behold, a hundred years ago scientists discovered that in *that* world, classical physics didn't apply. Common-sense rules work great up *here* where we live our day-to-day lives. But down *there* things work differently, in three basic ways.

1. Tiny objects (sub-atomic particles, or particles smaller than an atom) in the quantum world don't move the same way as large objects in the classical world. Up here, things move through space in a predictable pattern from here to there. Down there, they tend to jump around, appearing "here" a then suddenly appearing over "there" without seemingly moving along any observable path between two points. Now you see it, now you don't. Then you see it again. But now it's not "here." It's over "there."

Hence the term, *Quantum Leap*. How does it happen? No one knows. There are lots of theories, of course. But as of now we have to leave the question unanswered.

2. Up here where we live, things pretty much stay put whether or not we're watching them. A tree may or may not make noise when it falls in the forest and there's no one there to hear it, but barring fire, wind, and the chainsaw of a forester we pretty much figure that if we go away for a while and come back in a few days, the tree will still be there. It won't have gone away.

In the quantum world, that's not the case. Down there an object doesn't appear ("collapse" is the proper term) unless an observer is present to view (or "measure") it. And then, when it does appear, it's apt to take one of several forms, depending on the measuring device used to observe it. It's all about what we call the *Observer Effect*.

I know. It's weird. But trust me, that's what happens. The universe, in effect, has an "inside" and an "outside." Classical physics places us inside, a part of the whole. Quantum mechanics, however, demands an observer on the outside, making things happen simply by the act of observation.

How can the two be reconciled? By the existence of alternate universes into which the infinite quantum possibilities can collapse.

3. That leads the way to the most pertinent of all these strange, revolutionary ideas. This is the one that most concerns us in terms of OBEs. Before quantum physics came along we had pretty much determined that mind comes from brain. In other words, a physical lump of tissue, matter, and chemicals—the brain—produces electrical waves that generate thoughts and ideas in what we call our mind. As the philosopher René Descartes put it, "I think, therefore I am!" That kind of thing.

The new world of quantum reality, however, says that we deal with probabilities, not actualities. We can predict where and when something is *likely* to occur, but not precisely *how* it will occur.

Quantum mechanics is about possibilities that generate from us—the observers. We tend to observe what we *expect* to observe, and our methods of observation, the experiments we set up, determine our result. Look for a wave and you'll find a wave. Look for a particle and you'll find a particle.

The old way of thinking said we were pretty much spectators in a great, impersonal game called existence. Life is something that "happens" to us, usually, in the words of composer John Lennon, while we are busy making other plans.

We can't say that anymore. Instead, life is something that now seems to *proceed* from us. As observers, *we* are central to *its* existence, not the other way around.

And doesn't that idea play with your head!

Now let's take these three principles and, one by one, apply them to Out-of-Body Experiences.

1. Quantum Leaps

One way of understanding how sub-atomic particles such as electrons appear to "leap" from one place to another is that electrons aren't just particles. They are also waves. We have been taught to picture an electron as a tiny particle orbiting around the nucleus of an atom. If we look for it with an instrument designed to find it in that form, that's just what we discover.

But electrons have a secret identity. If you look for Clark Kent, that's who you'll find. But Clark Kent is also Superman. And electrons are also waves. So another way of picturing an electron is to picture a vague sort of cloud that inhabits a finite space.

Now comes the exciting part. The "space" this cloud inhabits actually consists of alternate universes that overlap each other at different "frequencies," for lack of a better word. If you were to somehow stand in a few of these parallel universes at the same time, and search for the "particle" identity of the electron, you would find it. It would appear as a miniscule dot in each overlapping universe.

So when we see an electron suddenly "leap" from "here" to "there," what we are actually seeing is the electron *as it appears in different places in overlapping universes!* In other words, we are actually *seeing*, or measuring, parallel universes! In each of these universes, different probabilities, or results, come to pass. In one universe a flipped coin is appearing heads up and your favorite football team elects to receive the kick-off. In another, it appears tails up, and they kick off.

Thus, in an infinite Multiverse, literally everything that *can* happen, *does* happen. But you, restricted by your five senses in this universe, observe only *one* of these results, so you think that's all that happens. The other "you," in a parallel universe, sees another result and feels *that* is all that happened.

But here's the point: When you move outside your senses you experience other realities—other universes—and observe a *different* outcome.

Which "you" is the real one?

Both are equally real! You inhabit all realities. It's only your five senses that create the illusion that this one is all there is.

This theory is called the *Many Worlds Hypothesis* and was developed by Hugh Everett back in the 1950s. Although it was never completely embraced by his colleagues during his relatively short lifetime, it is now growing in popularity because it's the only theory that ties up all the loose ends of current knowledge.

2. Observer-Based Causation

Now we move to the second big idea of quantum physics. Quantum physics insists that the observer—you—is very much connected to anything that happens. The observer—again, you—by the very act of observation, causes a wave of possibility to "collapse" into what we call material reality. The very act of seeing reality in a certain way brings that reality into existence in this particular universe. Trees are trees because, in this universe, that's what they look like to us.

But don't forget that there are both different universes and different entities within those universes. Here, in our world, a tree looks quite different to an amoeba, or even a fruit fly, than it does to you. If an ant could describe a maple tree, it would differ quite a bit from your description. Now imagine how the "you" from another, parallel, universe, would describe the same tree while observing its "cloud" of electrons as they appear over on the other side of the cosmic fence!

Once again, you are over "there," experiencing that tree, just as much as you are over "here." When you leave behind your five senses during an OBE, you are free to see reality from a completely different perspective.

No wonder things appear exotic at times!

3. Mind/Brain Dichotomy

Here in our world, brains pretty much rule. They are fantastic organs of protoplasm, cells, neuro-networks, and chemicals. It appears to us as though our brain is the originator of our minds—our thoughts and ideas. But that's an illusion. According to quantum physics, *mind* permeates and determines the course of matter.

This universe, and all universes, are the *result* of mind, not the *cause* of it. An observer brings about the collapse of a specific material result—here, there, and everywhere—in all universes, simultaneously.

Once again, as Sir James Jeans put it so eloquently, "The universe begins to look more like a great *thought* than like a great *machine*."

When we free our five senses from the single reality that appears to be our only choice in this perception realm, we begin to experience quite different landscapes, entities, and possibilities. Your brain will try to convince you that *this* is all there is—that *this* is the only reality. But now you know better. That's an illusion. There are infinite possibilities out there, created by universal Mind, or Consciousness, or God, or whatever you want to call it. They are yours to explore because your "mind" is a part of universal, creator, Mind. You're already there. With practice and intentional discipline, you can enter them all from this side.

Summary

In this chapter we have examined three lines of evidence that more than suggest OBEs are real:

ONE Legends, Myths, Religious Texts, and Oral History
TWO Eye Witness Testimonies
THREE Theories of Science

This is by no means a full-bore analysis. That would take at least another book, not a single chapter. But I hope it's enough to suggest that OBEs are not simply a quirky idea put forth by unstable minds, as I have often heard expressed even in polite conversation today.

There are surveys that point to the fact that some people will simply choose not to believe the evidence. They will go to their graves undecided or in flat-out denial of the reality of life after death and the continuation of any kind of human essence.

Those folk, though, have probably not made it this far into this book. If you're still with me you are no doubt anxious to cut to the chase. You are probably asking how you can achieve an OBE yourself.

If that is the case, it's time to turn to Part Two. I believe almost anyone with a serious intention and disciplined system can achieve their goal. It won't take years, either. If you work at it, in the first month of your practice you will achieve results. OBEs are not esoteric and kooky. They are normal. As we shall soon see, you've probably already had at least a partial experience.

Let's get practical. Let's get real. Let's get to work! Onward to *The Practice* of Out-of-Body Experience!

PART TWO

THE PRACTICE

THE PRACTICE

Consciously recognizing and personally experiencing our
nonphysical nature is a major step in our individual evolution.
William Buhlman in *Adventures Beyond the Body*

The Mystic's Journey

In shamanic cultures it's the task of the shaman to travel out of body to other worlds, experience new realities, and then bring knowledge back to the tribe in order to heal and restore balance. A journey simply for the purpose of seeking a recreational thrill is the height of irresponsibility, bordering on blasphemy. To experience a different reality and remain silent about it is simply not an option.

This highlights a personal problem for anyone who claims to have perceived a reality far different from the normal experience of the majority of 21st century people. What to do with such knowledge? Do we share it and risk ridicule, or keep quiet and stay anonymous?

On the one hand, to have such experiences and publish them for gain or the sake of ego-gratification is to risk trivializing a rich tradition that goes back thousands of years. On the other, to gain insight that can be of benefit to a human race which is in desperate need of spiritual underpinning, and then remain silent about it, might be even worse. According to shamanic tradition, the whole purpose of traveling out of body is to return with useful information.

Do we expect musicians to write glorious melodies and then hide them away in a drawer? Do we ask scientists to conduct life-altering experiments and then throw away the results? Should artists hide their work away so as not to draw attention to themselves by displaying it?

These are the kinds of questions that need to be answered before discussing experiences that fall outside traditional life expectations. But this is also why I intend to stick to my own perceptions. I will write about what I know. You are free to disregard anything you disagree with. That is as it should be. But just as I stand on the shoulders of those who have gone before me, whose experiences and testimonies have helped me in my life's journey, perhaps my experiences can be of some small help to you.

Be advised, though. I am not saying, "This is the way to do it—this is the way reality works!" My perceptions are undoubtedly flawed and subject to human misinterpretation. I do not claim to know "The Truth."

But I believe I have begun to glimpse the other side and learn something useful.

I moved to the woods upon retirement. I began a spiritual retreat that has lasted, so far, for ten wonderful years. It has, I think, produced something worth sharing.

That's the purpose of this book. That's my reason for writing it. For much of my life I, like most of us, let the technical necessities of daily existence drown out ancient voices that welled up from somewhere deep in my subconscious being, perhaps even in my DNA. In these busy days of media exposure and multi-tasking, it's almost inevitable.

I've been a member of the clergy for more than forty years. I was *supposed* to have a rich spiritual experience. It was part of my job description. But life is complicated. It's easy, even for ministers, to live day-to-day, putting off the search for answers to disturbing questions that intrude upon even the most peaceful moments of life.

Once in a while, however, something completely unbidden and unexpected happens to shake us out of our rut. Consider, for example, this entry from my journal:

August 24, 2012

It's 6:00 in the morning and even as I write these words I am beginning to doubt that what just happened did, indeed, happen. But I knew that would be the case. I even laughed as I reminded myself while it was going on that I would begin to question the experience when I "returned to my senses." But as the images begin to fade, and with full knowledge that words will be insufficient, here goes:

At 3:15 in the morning I am wide awake, having slept through the night without having to get up once. I decide to go into the living room, recline in my chair, and turn on some meditation music. I'm really not expecting anything except a quiet time. Rocky, our dog, comes in and begins his licking routine, which can be pretty distracting. Then I realize half an hour has gone by. I know this because the CD starts over and it's 25 minutes long. It skips a little at the beginning and I wonder if it has a scratch on it. But then my mental image suddenly changes.

I have a vision of myself lying on a mesh, rope-type hammock, very relaxed. My body has turned into something resembling butterfat, and is oozing down through the rope mesh. It's being strained, you might say, or sifted. As the body melts down through the mesh, what is left in the hammock is a bunch of tiny points of light. They have no form to speak of, but are clumped together. I guess the only image that comes close is to picture a school of fish, all swimming together—individuals, but collectively whole. I realize that I'm outside the school, watching it, but that somehow the lights are really me—my spiritual essence—my reality. With that thought I decide to unite my mind, on the outside, with the lights. I feel as if that's where it really belongs. Suddenly the lights come alive as one. We zoom off the hammock and begin to move. Without shock or concern, I realize I'm out of my body. I experience no random thoughts, no distractions. But at the same time I am somewhat amused. I realize that I will soon return to my body and try to convince myself that this is nothing other than self-hypnosis or some such thing. I find the whole exercise to be slightly ironic, in a patronizing sort of way, as if this is reality, but that poor, ignorant guy in the chair will soon think he is reality. With a sigh, much like a parent feels about the impossibility of correcting a wayward child, I move on.

First stop is the gazebo I built a few years ago. At the time I intended to use it for meditation. It overlooks our Medicine Wheel, a spiritual place that combines symbolic elements of Lakota and Hindu religious thought. I'm there in an instant, and am aware that it is surrounded by a tornado-like energy vortex. I can reach out and touch the sides, much like surfers do when they ride inside what they call a "tube" or curling wave.

But as powerful as this experience is, it's only a kind of refueling stop. The main event will happen down at the Medicine Wheel itself, and as soon as I think about it, I'm there. Its vortex is shaped a little differently than I imagined. It looks kind of like a chimenea. There is a round, bulbous-shaped area near the ground, and then it swirls into a kind of chimney at the top, much like the spires on Russian churches. There I meet someone, or something, that is very difficult to describe. It's not a "being," as such. It's more like a pillar, or tube, of light. It seems bright and, in contrast, I seem dark. (I guess anything would appear dark next to that light.)

I now seem to be watching from the outside, although taking part at the same time. Light and dark, the being and I, kind of swirl together, mingling.

I wonder if we will soon shoot out the top of the vortex together—but we don't. I really want to go. What's out there? What will I see?

But we stay within the confines of the Medicine Wheel vortex. I try, but to no avail. Then I'm back at the house. I'm aware of my body in the chair and try to reenter a few times, but each time I find an excuse to linger. I really don't want to go back and I fight the impulse. One of the things that makes me stay out is the sure and certain knowledge that I will soon find a perfectly good Freudian explanation for this whole experience. All I can do is shake my head and feel sorry for the poor chap in the chair who will be so hard to convince.

Finally I enter partway into my body in the chair, but I feel somehow lopsided. If asked where my center was located, I would have to say about two feet outside on the right. It's as though I was filled with water that sloshed over to one side. I manage to get up out of the chair, but it takes a while to readjust.

I decide to write this up quickly, before it fades. After all, it's probably just a case of self-hypnosis, right?

At this point I'm reminded of that wonderful line Dumbledore says to Harry Potter after Harry's near-death experience in the final book. Harry wants to know if what's happening to him is real or if it's just happening in his head. The old wizard replies, "Of course it's just happening in your head ... but why on earth should that mean that it is not real?"

What are my overall impressions of this experience?

Most of the time I was conscious of being in my body, but out of it at the same time. How is that possible? I really don't know. It's strange.

I have never experienced such meditative focus, without distraction, for that long a time. The experience took almost half an hour. I know this because the CD started up the second time and ended. I wasn't aware of the passing of time at all.

I have the impression that I was feeling a need to return, as if vacation was over but I didn't want it to end. Both the feeling of needing to get back home and the feeling of wanting to stay out were very real.

On the one hand, I never clearly "saw" my physical body from outside, but I was aware of it. It was almost as if I was in two places at once. On the other hand, I definitely "saw" what I can only call my spiritual or astral body at the Medicine Wheel with the being of light. I was an outside spectator yet I felt as though I was there. I suppose if anyone would have come up to me and asked where "I" was, I would have said, "Right here in my chair." But I definitely felt as though I were down at the Medicine Wheel.

The overall feeling was one of peace, yet at the same time, exciting—a determination to explore.

Somehow it felt like this was a watershed moment in my life. There have been a few of those in the past, but I wasn't able to articulate them, in some cases even recognize them, until later. With this one, I knew. But I don't know how I knew.

Back to Earth

What really happened on that day so many years ago? Was it just a dream? Did I imagine the whole thing? Was it an elaborate hallucination—a figment of my imagination?

Part of me, the rational part that has kept me (mostly) out of trouble and been responsible for whatever successes I have had in life over the last seven decades, wants to ignore the whole experience. But there's another part, one that I find I simply can't disregard, that won't accept any of those explanations. Indeed, that part of me actually wants to tell the world about it in hopes that someone, somewhere, will benefit from it.

In the years since 2012 I have had plenty of time to research what back then I thought was a unique experience. I am also the veteran of enough OBEs to have discovered how blind I was for most of my life. Once I started researching the subject it didn't take long to discover that thousands of people now living have had similar Out-of-Body Experiences. If you study historical documents you will soon learn that millions of people have had them. In some cultures OBEs have been expected, deliberately sought, and considered to be an important part of both human and tribal development.

Some members of the contemporary scientific community have now begun to get on board. They have learned that when we start to consider other realms that bubble up from the complex mathematical equations of quantum physics, we soon discover a surprising fact: Life as we normally experience it is an illusion. Nothing is really as it seems. Indeed, with increasing frequency, the voice of the prophet is sounding forth not from pulpits and places of worship but from the lecture halls and science labs of academia.

A Minister's Quest

When my wife and I retired in 2009 we did so with a specific agenda. It was much the same as that of Henry David Thoreau. We wanted to live deliberately. We went on retreat. Not for a weekend or even a month or two. We wanted to live that way for a period of years to see what would happen. Ignoring the accepted theory preached by the U.S.-based AARP magazine that retired people need to surround themselves with friends lest they get depressed, we decided to live away from the distraction other human beings might impose on us. Instead, we wanted to find God. We wanted to live in a state of meditation.

For me, ministry has always been more about spiritual growth than social service. I wanted to experience God. But, largely because of my passion, organized religion has not been really satisfying for me. I never found a way of thinking or practicing group religion that did more than explain and neatly codify what passes for spiritual experience.

I've run the gamut. After a full-blown fundamentalist conversion I served time as an Evangelical, a Charismatic, a main-line conservative, and a flaming liberal. I've studied Zen Buddhism, Hinduism, Daoism, various Indian religions, classical philosophy and New Age spiritualities. I've meditated, mediated, illuminated, contemplated, and postulated. I've taught more seminars than I can possibly remember, written eleven books and been a college professor, teaching in the fields of comparative religion, cross-cultural studies, and instrumental music. I've preached more than six thousand sermons, led countless Bible studies, and hosted a drive-time religious radio program.

After all this you would think a person would have the sense to call himself an expert and retire into a season of contentment and relaxation while contemplating a life well spent.

But it didn't work that way. I never intended to give God a rest. Like the story of Jacob found in the book of Genesis, I intended to wrestle with God, shouting out loud, "I will not let you go until you bless me!"

In doing so I discovered that the universe sometimes conspires to meet us half-way on our journey towards spiritual growth. A few years into my retirement I was invited to Cornwall to present a talk about the roots of world religions. As I wrote in my book, *Supernatural Gods*, while in England I fulfilled a cherished dream to visit a small church in Fenny Compton where some of my ancestors, clergy associated with the Church of England, used to preach. I had a chance to stand in their pulpit, look out at the same sanctuary that greeted them on Sabbath mornings, and think about what kind of people they were. I wondered if they ever thought about a possible descendant who turned out to be me.

Then, while exploring the stained glass windows they saw each and every Sunday morning, I came across a theme I had never before seen portayed in this medium. It was a picture of Jacob, wrestling with God. Beneath it were the words, "There wrestled a man with him." It was an artistic depiction of the same scripture verse that has inspired the quest of my retirement years. My ancestors saw it each and every week.

This personal story has a purpose. To seek true reality, rather than the illusion of it that surrounds our waking life, to "wrestle" with God or Spirit, is to discover an obvious truth: You cannot wrestle alone. In deep meditation we enter into a dialogue, a conversation with God, with the supernatural, with that which is greater than ourselves—a higher power. And the supernatural responds in ways which, in my case at least, took me all the way to England in order to illustrate its presence, both in my life and those who eventually produced me.

Here in Part Two we're going to move from learning *about* OBEs to actually experiencing them. There are "wrestling" techniques which might prove helpful. There are disciplines to learn. Hopefully, by describing the path I took, it will help you find your own. There is no single way. Everyone's life is unique. This is not an inclusive instruction manual. My experience will not be the same as yours. But perhaps, just perhaps, it will strike a note that you will hear—a note that will lead you to experience the music of the spheres.

Let's begin at the beginning...

SIX

FIRST EXPLORATIONS

There, right in front of our house, I received the shock of my life.
While concentrating as best I knew how, I took the step
that has probably changed me forever.
Jim Willis in *The Dragon Awakes*

Breaking Free from Illusion

How do you begin to break free of the five senses that have stood you in good stead for your whole life? How do you experience consciousness while outside your physical body? How do you separate the "I" who *has* a body from the body it "has?"

In order to begin to break free of your sensory prison and what I like to call the "Great Illusion," try this thought experiment.

Look at the book you now hold in your hand. Is it right-side up?

"Of course it is," you say. "How else could I read it?"

The truth is that your brain is playing a trick on you even as you read. The book may be right-side up in your hand, but since light travels in straight lines and the entrance to your eye is very small, the light image of the bottom edge of the book actually enters your eye from the bottom and registers behind your retina at the top of your brain's screen. Conversely, the top of the book is cast at the bottom of the screen.

To live in a world that appears upside-down, however, would cause a lot of confusion. So your brain has learned to turn things right-side up so as to make sense. You're not aware of it, of course. It's just one of those things you learned to do when you were much too young to remember.

But take it one step further. Consider the situation from another point of view. Does the book appear to be solid? That, too, is an illusion. Actually, the book is made up of subatomic particles, constantly moving through space and never at rest. It is energy in motion. Mass and energy are the same thing. Einstein taught us that energy is equal to mass times the speed of light squared (E=mc²). So nothing is solid at all. It just appears to be. That's the way our senses force us to experience it.

Now let's view the book through the lens of time.

As we evolved we learned to perceive things as they appear to exist during the relatively short time span of a human life. But bury the book in the earth, come back a thousand years from now, and try to dig it up. You will discover that what it appeared to be when you covered it with dirt was only one physical manifestation in a constantly transforming journey that lasts forever.

Then there's the philosophical level. Does the reality of the book consist of material elements at all? Is it paper and ink, or is it the essence of ideas that are written on the paper with the ink? In other words, does the book continue after its physical manifestation is destroyed? Are the paper and ink simply one incarnation of eternal ideas that will live on as long as someone remembers them? Are the ideas the reality, or the printed words that describe the ideas?

What we've just done is to identify three levels of reality when it comes to books: the physical reality of the paper and ink, the symbolic representation of the words themselves, and the ideas the words conjure up. Perhaps the words *body* (the paper and ink*), soul* (the choice and style of the words employed), and *spirit* (the ideas expressed), come closer to the truth. In this case we can visualize the book as what theologians call a trinity. How does this pertain to the illusion of its three levels of reality?

Body

Energy cannot be manufactured or destroyed. It just changes form. So on a material level the book was once an acorn and then a tree. It might someday become soil that nurtures a flower that produces energy for a honeybee, transferred into nourishment for a reader who will someday hold a book in her hand. The process continues as long as there is a Cosmos. It's called reincarnation.

Soul

What about the words written on the book's pages? They comprise languages which sometimes borrow from each other to express similar ideas. These ideas comprise the meaning, the personality, or *soul*, of the book. Every book is thus different from every other book, just as human souls differ from one another.

The point of *words* is to express the *thoughts* of the writer. But in doing so, they express his or her personality as well.

Spirit

Ideas are illusive, too, but they consist of the *spirit* behind the words. Sometimes ideas are best expressed intuitively. Intuitive understanding is what makes jokes funny, for instance. The humor is in the paradox—the unexpected, sudden realization. If you have to explain why something is funny, it ceases to be humorous. Words are fine, but they have limitations. Their usefulness lies in the fact that both the speaker and the hearer have similar experiences that will conjure up familiar images.

Piercing the Veil

Here's the point of this lengthy exercise. The book we have been considering serves as a metaphor for your life. If a simple concept like "book" is so difficult to pin down, what about you?

You, too, are a trinity. You consist of a physical body, a soul (a personality that makes you unique), and an eternal spirit (an essence that is the very spark of existence).

Because of the Great Illusion, because nothing is as it seems, our senses play tricks with reality in order to keep us focused and grounded. But don't hold it against them. They mean no harm. Over the millennia of the existence of life on Earth they have had to learn to organize, categorize, and even deceive on occasion. It's their way of providing stability to what would otherwise be a chaotic life.

Thus, life *is* an illusion. Nothing is really as it seems. But sometimes seeing through the Great Illusion helps to pacify the warring emotions that hinder our understanding of reality.

Choosing to act based on what you *believe* to be real rather than life's illusion is often called acting on *faith*. But be careful! Are you sure that something is true just because you believe it? How do you know that the tenets of your world view, for instance, represent something real? How can you be sure science offers something trustworthy to believe in? Perhaps it is merely an elaborate game of systemization played by our senses. What if our perception of reality is simply a matter of our senses trying to organize that which doesn't really exist by turning it into something believable?

See how complicated this gets? Your life is like a multi-layer cake. You exist on many levels.

Beliefs and Knowns

Experience is everything. It turns *beliefs* into *knowns*. You can express a belief in something without really knowing for sure that it is real.

I've always believed in England, for instance. I had good evidence. I've seen pictures. I've had English friends who told me about it. I've seen it on maps and even watched Diana's wedding on TV.

But I didn't know for sure if it was real. The whole England thing could have been an elaborate hoax perpetrated by a conglomerate of people who joined together to deceive me.

Improbable? Sure.

Likely? Not very.

But I had never been there, so how could I know for sure?

Then I went.

Now I know.

It's as simple as that. My *belief*, strong as it was, turned into a *known*. I no longer had only an intellectual concept of England. I now knew what it looked like, what it smelled like, what it tasted like, and how it felt.

That's what we need to do with OBEs. We can *believe* in them. We can apply all the evidence we have just discussed about our lives being analogous to a multi-layered cake consisting of both physical and spiritual components. But in order to *know* OBEs are real we need to experience one.

That's what happened to me.

August 16, 2012

Was it an OBE or did I imagine it? While meditating, my mind was jumping around. First I tried to imagine my astral body leaving my physical body. I tried to envision the Medicine Wheel, the front porch—anywhere away from my body. I affirmed to myself that I was a multi-dimensional being capable of moving between those dimensions. All the usual stuff. I was getting frustrated. Nothing was working.

Then, for just a minute, something happened. I felt myself drawn backwards, away from my body. The feeling of motion was very obvious. I felt vibrations throughout my body and was aware of a copper taste behind my teeth. Suddenly, completely unbidden, I pictured myself as a 20 year old. I looked just the same as I used to look, and felt strong and thin. I had full awareness of this image and played with it a minute, knowing that I hadn't planned for this, and began to wonder if this was, indeed, an OBE. I thought for a moment that if I could talk to this kid, he would make different choices and live a different life.

But then I started to fly (not really "fly," but it's the only word that works, "zoom" might be better) towards the sun. My hands were at my side and I was moving through space. I wasn't at all worried. I wanted to plunge into the sun because I felt that if I did, it would burn away all my guilt, worries, and fears, leaving only the pure essence of the real me. I looked forward to it, but before I got there I felt an urge to empty my full bladder. (The curse of old age!) I felt very heavy, however, and had to wait awhile before I could get up out of the chair.

Well, what's the verdict? Was this indeed an OBE? If it was, it was not what I expected. Here are the positives and negatives:

Positive I never intended to picture myself as a 20-year-old kid in the prime of life. That was totally unexpected. Also unexpected was the feeling of being drawn backwards away from my body. That has happened once before, but not as pronounced as this. The part about talking to my younger self and changing my life was the farthest thing from my mind. Also, the copper taste behind my teeth intrigues me.

Later: In regards to the copper taste I had, I recently searched the Internet to learn what alchemists had to say about copper in general. Interestingly, a number of sites, all seemingly quoting the same source that I could not verify, had this to say:

> *"Copper is known as a good conductor of energy, as well as a balancing metal that works with the flow of projective and receptive energies.*
> *Copper is known to Shamans and Healers to be a metal that balances the body's polarities, thereby removing blockages which are responsible for illness or imbalance… Copper can be seen as having a soul as well as a body, and the Art of Alchemy can be defined as 'the liquefaction of the body and the separation of the soul from the body, seeing that copper, like a man, has a soul and a body.'"*

Negative I can honestly say that except for brief seconds here and there, I was always conscious of being in my chair and was almost always trying to decide if this was real or imaginary. It wouldn't take much to convince me that I dreamed up the whole thing—but that just doesn't *feel* right. I guess only time and practice will tell. At least I'm encouraged.

Analysis

That entry in my journal describes the first time I experienced something akin to actually leaving my body. I had earlier experienced what I call visions, but my history of Out-of-Body Experiences began that day. What had I done to get to that point? Perhaps my preparations can serve as a guide to others.

How to Engage an OBE

William Buhlman is one of the most experienced out-of-body practitioners teaching today. His book, *Adventures Beyond the Body: How to Experience Out-of-Body Travel,* is a classic. In his workshops, usually a week long, he insists that anyone can experience an OBE if they are willing to put in the work required for at least 30 days. Soon after I experienced my first OBE I enrolled in one of his seminars at the Monroe Institute in Virginia.

The late Robert Monroe, founder of the Institute, is the man who introduced OBEs into the public arena. Indeed, he was the one who coined the term, "Out-of-Body Experience," or OBE. In his books *Journeys Out of Body, Far Journeys*, and *Ultimate Journey*, he recounts his unexpected discovery of out-of-body travel, his personal experiments, and his discoveries along the way.

With the possible exception of a certain former Christian minister who is writing this book, he was probably the least likely candidate that anyone could have imagined for such a task. His work in radio and sound techniques concerned research and analysis. It was about as far from mysticism and out-of-body travel as one could possibly imagine. But it prepared him for his life's work. He was one of the first to bring strict scientific protocols to the study of what was, up to then, a field identified with the paranormal and supernatural. Monroe, in a radical departure from anything resembling what is now called New Age thinking, insisted that if out-of-body travel was possible and real it needed to be studied and analyzed in a manner congruent with any other physical phenomenon. He insisted our minds needed to be employed as well as our intuition. "Body asleep but mind awake" became his mantra, along with another favorite saying: "We are more than our bodies."

The first of his great contributions to the field was the invention of Hemi-Sync music. Here is how it is described on the website of the Monroe Institute:

"Hemi-Sync® is a scientifically based and clinically proven 'audio-guidance' technology that uses sound to influence brain wave activity. This patented, and highly sophisticated technology is backed by over 50 years of research.

Hemi-Sync® is an audio-guidance process that works through the generation of complex, multilayered audio signals, which act together to create a resonance that is reflected in unique brain wave forms characteristic of specific states of consciousness. The result is a focused, whole-brain state known as hemispheric synchronization, or 'Hemi-Sync®,' where the left and right hemispheres are working together in a state of coherence. As an analogy, lasers produce focused, coherent light. Hemi-Sync® produces a focused, coherent mind, which is an optimal condition for improving human performance."

www.monroeinstitute.org/catalog/hemi-sync%C2%AE

Hemi-Sync® CDs are now readily available from multiple sources on the Internet. The one I have used for years is called *Sleeping Through the Rain*, produced by Monroe Products. Most shamanic practitioners swear by traditional drumming CDs. The monotonous but powerful rhythms produced by experienced drummers do, indeed, mimic the classic drumming used by shamans for thousands of years. I have some of these recorded with Hemi-Sync® technology and use them. But for some reason I keep going back to my old faithful, *Sleeping Through the Rain*. Maybe it's just habit, but it works for me.

Monroe's second great contribution lives on as well. It's the Monroe Institute. Dedicated to "further the experience and exploration of consciousness, expanded awareness, and discovery of self through technology, education, research, and development," the Institute played host to more than 20,000 seekers during its first 30 years of existence.

In 1994, the Wall Street Journal reported that the Intelligence and Security Command of the United States Army had been sending personnel to the Institute to study remote viewing. That's hardly the stuff of woo-woo New Age mysticism.

Some Zen Buddhist adepts with a lifetime of practice insist that students who had been through the *Gateway Program* at the Institute, its initial program for beginning students, could attain meditation states that normally took thirty years or so of traditional meditation practice. (You can find out more about the Monroe Institute online at www.monroeinstitute.org/)

Obviously there is more to OBE study than meets the eye. After reading William Buhlman's book and discovering the work of the Monroe Institute I couldn't resist the opportunity when I learned he would be presenting a week-long workshop on OBEs at the Institute.

It turned out to be quite an intense experience. I met some great folks, some of whom I still hear from occasionally. The Institute itself is located in a beautiful, rural, Virginia location. The staff was wonderful, the food fantastic, and the atmosphere positive. Bill was an experienced presenter and a gifted speaker. It should have been a terrific time.

But it didn't work for me. And it was all my fault.

Maybe I had expected too much. Maybe I was in a different place than the others. Perhaps, in an ego-centric way, I grew weary of hearing variations on a theme as, one by one, participants shared the initial OBE experiences they encountered throughout the week. Maybe, as a former minister who has led too many group experiences, I was just too blasé to participate in good faith.

But the truth is, I think the problem was psychologically deeper than that. After 7 decades of intense introspection I have come to realize that I don't function well in groups. I'm a loner.

I've made two solo cross country bicycle trips from the Pacific Ocean to the Atlantic, and one from Florida to Massachusetts. I've hiked for miles by myself on the Appalachian Trail. I've spent a lot of time alone in the woods. I don't know why. There are groups that sponsor these things. They ensure safety and sociability. But I don't enjoy them. It's just the way I'm wired.

It's not that I don't like people. I do. I can be as social as the next guy, although I must confess that I get rather bored at parties unless the conversation moves beyond a discussion of the weather or what someone named Beyoncé wore on her last trip down the red carpet.

So when I set out on a quest to discover whether or not I could actually move my conscious self out of the confines of my material body, I just naturally followed my own lead at my own pace in my own way. That's what I've always done. I wanted to trust my own instincts and move at my own pace. I wanted to make my own discoveries and translate my own beliefs, such as they were, into my own, personal *knowns*.

Now, you may be different than me. You may function much better in a community setting. You may do very well in a group of searchers who share a common goal while feeding off each other's energy.

If so, I can recommend without qualification a William Buhlman seminar and a week at the Monroe Institute in Virginia or one of their many satellite locations. They both are excellent resources. It will probably cost a few thousand dollars, between fees and travel expenses, but I assure you that it will be well worth it.

If, however, you would like to work toward the personal freedom of an OBE, hoping to perceive a reality totally outside your normal experience while proceeding at your own pace in familiar surroundings, there are alternatives to pursue.

Some shamanic practitioners insist you need to enlist the skills of drummers. Others swear it requires hallucinogens such as ayahuasca, peyote, or psychedelics. I don't know anything about these except that they do, indeed, have a long and rich history, in some cases going back as long as 40,000 years or so. Graham Hancock's book, *Supernatural*, listed at the end of this book, is a good place to start if that interests you.

But for me, the safest and simplest method involves meditation, a reliable CD player with a good set of earphones, and a dependable set of Hemi-Sync® CDs. It's an inexpensive mixture of new technology and ancient techniques.

First Steps

1. Make the Decision

I wish I could promise an easy path, but make no mistake: You are setting out to do something that goes against the grain of evolution. Our species developed within a system that produced individual identity—a singular experience of uniqueness.

We can't see into someone else's mind and brain. Each of us is an experiment of one. Two people, no matter how close they may be, can witness an event and come away with different impressions of it. I don't hear the same music you hear, even though we may be sitting next to each other at a concert. The sun rises differently for you than for me because we both draw on different recollections and memories of similar sunrises.

When our lives are over and we rejoin the Source in perfect unity, we may discover that was the whole purpose of life. In perfect Unity there is no uniqueness, no difference of opinion. Maybe the reason we are alive at all is that each of us desired an experience of individuality. The only way to fulfill that desire was to journey from the Akashic Field out here to what I sometimes call our Perception Realm.

However we think about it and whatever the truth may be, the fact remains that we were physically born into an environment that forces us to become expressions of uniqueness and individuality. When it comes to teaching ego development, it's hard to imagine a better school than life in this perception realm.

So when you decide to return to the source of all that is, you are seeking to move outside a highly evolved system that has molded and shaped you over the course of your whole lifetime. Ever since you drew your first breath your senses have been teaching you their interpretation of the nature of reality.

Now you want to move outside your sensory input. It takes more than a simple decision. It takes discipline and work:

Your material body is a mass of seething energy. You are seeking perfect peace.

Your mind is a jumbled mess of thoughts, ideas, memories, and hopes. You are seeking quiet, focused awareness.

Your attention is constantly drawn to signals emanating from your environment. You are seeking one-pointed, focused attention on eternal stillness.

Your experience tells you that your past is moving through your present into your future. You are seeking only the now.

See how difficult this can be? It will take more than a simple decision. But a simple decision is where it has to start. Make that decision.

2. Stick to It

Once you have made your decision you need to stick to it. When I first read William Buhlman's *Adventures Beyond the Body*, I was struck by the fact that he insisted anyone could experience an OBE if he or she was willing to apply themselves to deliberate meditation for a period of thirty days. I decided to try it. It worked, but it took the full thirty days. If I had given up after 28 or 29 days I wouldn't be writing this book.

For those who have never practiced intentional meditation, it's a lot harder than it looks. To an outsider it appears as though you're just sitting there with your eyes closed. Easy, right?

Try it sometime.

Your mind goes crazy. It rambles on in stream-of-consciousness thoughts that are funny if you decide to deliberately track them.

You decide you are going to clear your mind of all thoughts. And you do it. For about ten seconds. Then you remember something you forgot to do. So you file it away. That reminds you of a phone call you need to make. Wasn't that a funny thing your spouse said to you today? It was similar to something you once heard while you were driving through the town where you used to live. Whatever happened to that little house you always admired on the corner of first and third? Someone lived there who you haven't thought about in years. What was his name? His mother and your mother were friends. Didn't they move away while you were in High School? He once wrote in your yearbook that he would never forget those times in study hall. But you can't remember his name. Study hall! That brings back some tense moments. But back to meditating. Concentrate! There. Your mind is empty again. What was that phone call you needed to remember to make...?

And on and on it goes. You strive for peace and stillness. How do you strive? By not striving. It's very Zen-like, isn't it? Meditation is hard work. But if you work hard at it, you fail. You've got to relax.

It's a battle you can't win. All you can do is continue to try. There's a reason folks say they "practice" meditation. It takes practice. It takes consistency. You need to stick to it.

3. Develop a System

For me, I soon learned I needed to develop a system if I was going to get anywhere. This was important to me and I needed to intentionally treat it as such. That means it needed to take priority. If I just tried to fit in an hour here or there when I had some free time it was an indication that it wasn't high on my priority list. You don't just "fit in" things that are important to you. You schedule them. I decided to determine a time during the day when I was most physically and mentally wired to meditate, set that time aside, and never, ever, let anything interfere.

For me that time was (don't laugh!) 3:00 in the morning. I had discovered that, for some reason, I was always awake at that time, anyway. I was usually rested after some six hours of sleep, but not ready to get up and start the day.

Now, am I saying you need to set your alarm for 3:00 every morning?

No! That time worked for me. But your body rhythms are not the same as mine. You shouldn't set your alarm at all when it comes to meditating. Your body and work schedule will tell you what time is best for you. If you try to meditate when your mind is wired to start the day you will fail to find any real peace. If you try when your body is tired you will fall asleep. The trick is to find that time when your mind is at peace and your body is at rest without being overly tired. For me, that was at 3:00 in the morning.

I soon discovered that I needed some help, though. I am an active, left-brained thinker. My chattering monkey brain cuts loose when I allow it off the leash.

That's where Hemi-Sync® CDs came into the picture. I have a number of them. They really help me focus.

It was also important for me to deliberately get up and out of bed and go to a dedicated chair in a different room in the house.

Some people swear by meditating in bed as they drift off to sleep. Others claim that what works best for them is to light a candle in a dedicated meditation room, sit in a specific posture, or listen to guided meditation CDs.

Try it. If that works for you, fine. You need to find your own system. Mine was to wake up naturally about 3:00 in the morning, move to a different room, sit in a specific chair, and listen to specific music. The fact that I woke up naturally within five minutes of 3:00 in the morning, every morning, without fail for 30 days, either means I had developed a habit or I had help. I used to think it was habit. Now I'm not so sure. I've come to believe that once we start intentionally seeking help from the Source of All That Is, "unseen angels" become available and willing to help.

4. Focus, Focus, Focus!

Now things start to get a bit more subtle. You need to visualize what you are doing. That sounds like self-hypnosis. Maybe, to a certain extent, it is. Ideally you are trying for a completely open, receptive mind. But that's not easy to achieve. You will probably discover that you need, at least in the beginning, some kind of mental crutch. You may find it helpful to picture yourself visiting a room or natural setting with which you are very familiar. Maybe it will help to imagine yourself sitting up and rolling away from your body.

In his workshops, William Buhlman sometimes passes around a thick piece of rope that people can hold in their hands, developing a tactile memory so that during their meditation period they can mentally "climb" up the rope and away from their physical bodies. You'll need to develop a set of images that work for you.

Are these all "props?" Yes. Do they serve as a mental crutch? Of course. But when you're trying to walk after a long time of nursing a broken foot, sometimes you need a crutch to help you get strong enough to walk on your own.

Don't forget. Your mind-connection with universal consciousness has been "broken" for a long time, trained to think it is trapped in a physical body. You're now learning to walk. Accept the crutch. It will help you along until you get stronger. You won't always need it.

5. Stay Calm

Eventually there will come a time when something unexpected happens. It won't last for more than a moment or two, but when it does you will somehow know in a flash that you have seen a glimmer of something outside your experience. In one terrible, wonderful, awe-inspiring minute you will know, somehow, that you have experienced leaving your body, or at least have felt something akin to an OBE. It will really impress you. When that happens you will probably try to re-live or recreate that experience next time you meditate. That's a trap! Every experience is unique and different. Trying to induce an OBE by remembering an experience you have already had is to limit yourself to that one experience.

Am I saying you need to create a "prop" to help you get out and then ignore that prop when it comes up again?

Yes. Don't dwell on it. As I said before, it's very Zen-like.

I'm not trying to be difficult or deliberately evasive here. It's just that words fail. If you focus enough, and keep at it, something will happen that you can't explain.

When you achieve perfect stillness, or something very close to it, you will, for that moment, be open and receptive to Universal Consciousness. You'll recognize it. You'll feel it.

And in that moment you will perceive *Universal* consciousness rather than *individual* consciousness. You will be free from the confines of your sense-oriented body. You will have experienced your first OBE.

Once it happens you will, quite naturally, be excited. Try to remain calm. The quickest way to snap back into the waking reality of your body is to start analyzing what just happened. The surest way to come back home is to exclaim, "Hey! I'm out!"

If you do get excited, and everybody does, don't be disappointed when you snap out of it and "come to your senses." It happened once. That's good. It will happen again. Stay calm and do your best. Nobody's perfect.

6. Keep a Journal

For me, this was the hardest step, but also the most important. Once I had experienced a brief moment of timelessness I wanted to luxuriate in it. The last thing I wanted to do was write it down. But I have found that without my journal I would by now have forgotten most of what I experienced. It is very important to record your experiences as soon as you can while they are still fresh in your mind. Please do it. You'll never regret it even if, at the time, it's a real pain.

Final Thoughts on New Beginnings

We've begun. We're on our way. There's much more to come. But let's concentrate on three more things.

First of all, what does an OBE feel like? I said a minute ago that you would definitely feel something. But what?

Here we go again. It's hard to put into words. Let me go back again to random samplings from my own journal to see how I described it when the feeling was still pristine and new. Each of the following paragraphs is from a separate entry:

I felt myself become instantly peaceful inside. A bright, white, hot light seemed to enter my body through an opening at the top of my head. Slowly it spread through my entire body. I seemed to be inside a swirling, tornado-like vortex of energy. I felt a very real sensation of rotating in a counterclockwise direction. I was moving so fast that my physical body seemed to be pushed to the outside, much as a spinning whirlpool centrifugally pushes water out to the vortex around it. But I was at peace, in the middle. All around me was motion, but my central core was at rest in the middle of it all.

Although I don't feel as though I leave my body, I am conscious of being aware that my body is in the chair but that I am standing up, talking to something or someone who is most definitely a real entity. But I don't have the faintest recollection what he or she looks like, or even if it is a he or a she.

For a moment I had an image in my mind of flying. It wasn't that I was in an airplane, but rather that I *was* an airplane. I distinctly saw the right wing. But it only lasted a moment.

I sensed a slowing down of time and movement, so I asked for clarity and settled down to see what would happen. Out of the vortex around me there slowly rose a tube that seemed to be the universe, or material reality. I simply haven't the words to describe it. It eventually turned into some kind of funnel. I had the impression that I was watching time unfold, carrying with it the entire material universe. I felt that I could step into it at any time and experience a life within the unfolding dimension of space and the earth, or perhaps many earths—many worlds. It slowly revolved around and around, immense, but small at the same time. I was somehow in command of the process. It was bigger than me but I was larger than the process, watching it unfold as if in slow motion and, immense as it appeared from the inside, it was smaller than me. I felt the urge to return to my body, but even this could be controlled. I wonder if I was not only out of body, but out of time itself. I wonder if I was experiencing the universe from the outside, created as a teaching tool of experience into which we could dip whenever we wanted to or felt the need. It was immense, but I could almost hold it in my hand.

Second, what about fear? You're doing something you've never done before. You live in a culture that, for better or for worse, emphasizes fear of death. Hell and damnation have been used to intimidate and force cooperation. Zombies and horror films are sources of entertainment. Waking in terror from one nightmare is enough to make you afraid. It's only natural to fear that which is unknown.

I'll have more to say about this in later chapters, but for now, try to put your fears behind you. Love is a universal constant throughout our cosmos and all its suburbs. In my case, I find it helpful to focus on the words of the Bible at this point. Whether or not you accept the idea of divinely inspired religious texts, there is wisdom here:

"Perfect love casts out fear!"

1st John 4:18

Third, how do you handle your doubts after an OBE? They are inevitable. As soon as you find yourself back on familiar ground you will undoubtedly begin to think that what you have just experienced was a self-induced fantasy, that it could not be real.

Expect it. It is perfectly normal. But there are evidential threads that you cannot ignore. The hardest thing for someone who has never experienced an OBE to understand is what it *feels* like. Almost everyone who is experienced in out-of-body travel insists that it feels more real "out there" than "in here."

"It's so real!" they exclaim. "Everything is so much more vivid!" "It felt as though *that* was the reality, not *this*!"

These claims are easy to dispute. They are purely subjective, after all. If someone wants physical proof, feelings simply don't matter—except to those who have actually experienced an OBE!

How do you explain the color pink to someone who is color blind?

You can't.

We live in a world of people who, if not color blind, are OBE blind. Accept it. That's just the way it is.

But even harder to convince will be your own sense of doubt. So record everything in your journal, no matter how trivial it seems. You will soon discover that you have recorded things that cannot be explained. Events, sights, memories, things that you didn't know about, sights you've never experienced—all are a mine of information that, upon reflection, will convince you that something real happened that you cannot explain.

I'll have much more to say about this. But for now, suspend judgment and commit all your impressions to writing. Make it as detailed as you can. You'll be glad you did.

The Bottom Line

We've covered a great deal of information in this chapter. My advice is to pause here and try to put some of it into practice. Although you may not feel like you're ready, you now have enough background to begin your practice and experience your first OBE, if only briefly. When you do, we can continue together. Give it plenty of time. There's no rush.

Let's recap:
- Make the Decision
- Stick To It
- Develop a System
- Focus, Focus, Focus!
- Stay Calm
- Keep a Journal

Don't analyze too much yet. Just experience. Whatever happens, we'll try to cover it in the next few chapters. Peace, and happy journeying!

SEVEN
STAYING GROUNDED

The idea of a deep dimension is a perennial insight:
the world we observe is not the ultimate reality. It is the manifestation
of a reality that lies beyond the plane of our observation.
Ervin Laszlo in *Science and the Akashic Field*

"Be Still, and Know..."

One of my favorite Bible verses is Psalm 46:10—"Be still, and know..." I have come to believe that stillness is the key to success and happiness. I rarely practice it. But I believe it.

Every vortex has a still point at its center. The winds of a hurricane may wreak havoc, but at the very center of the storm lies the eye, the point of stillness. Sometimes our lives resemble hurricanes. Events, ideas, and thoughts swirl around us, most of them seemingly out of our control. The trick is to find the still point in the center. Only there can we "take leave of our senses" and venture out of body.

If you took some time off when you finished the last chapter, and followed my advice to devote some time and effort to engaging your first OBE, you probably learned during your meditation time that your inner life is a lot more hectic than you care to think about.

If, however, you are like me, you probably plowed right ahead from that chapter to this, figuring that you want to finish the whole book before you sit down to meditate.

That, in itself, illustrates the problem most of us face in this hectic and busy life. We just don't understand the depths of our frenetic existence. We multitask ourselves to death. Literally.

We jump from activity to activity. Our attention span is shortening. We constantly check our social media feed. We have trouble sitting down and reading books, much preferring TV or digital media. Our politics come in sound bites. Our wisdom derives from snippets no bigger than a bumper sticker. The thought of being stuck in a waiting room with nothing to do terrifies us. We even panic at red lights when they seem to take too long to turn green. We are, indeed, a society on multitasking steroids.

Forgotten is the leisurely wagon ride to town. Long walks have been replaced by aerobic workouts, our ear buds firmly in place. I'm even old enough to remember the scandal that broke out when classical music stations began playing a single movement of a four-movement symphony because they thought no one wanted to sit still for the full, forty-minute, complete performance of a work by Beethoven or Brahms. And that was more than 30 years ago!

Have you watched an old movie lately? Did it drag? Were there long moments when nothing happened, or the camera seemed to focus interminably on an actor's face?

I don't mean to condemn, or even criticize. (Well, maybe a little. But I do it in love!) Those too young to remember these things will think I'm sounding old fashioned. Perhaps they're right. But older people will need no reminder.

And it's not just a generational thing. Those of us who grew up with only three channels on the TV have a hard time remembering what we did with our time all day. Our parents who grew up only with radio said the same thing about us. It may begin seeming like an age gap, but us old-timers now check our Facebook feed first thing every morning just like our kids.

Life winds up. It rarely winds down unless we make it do so.

When Barb and I retired we wanted to return to a simpler time. It only partially happened. We may live in the woods and not own a cell phone, but we still have high-speed Internet service. We watch more TV, not less. We cut our cable, but are still addicted. Thanks to our computer we are more connected to old friends now then we were even ten years ago.

And that's a good thing. I guess.

But we quickly discovered how hard it is to slow down our internal clock. Days go by when we don't see or hear anyone out here, surrounded by the peace and quiet we both crave. We talk more softly, we move slower, and are amazed how loud and boisterous things are when we make a weekly trip to town for groceries. But our souls are still wound up pretty tight. And that's after nine years.

We could sit out on the porch and watch animals all day. But we don't.

We had to really work at it when we decided to spend a few moments reading aloud every morning after breakfast. Now, even that delightful habit is challenged.

At our age, relaxing with a good book sometimes seems more a chore than a privilege. So, thanks to our fire stick, we binge-watch TV just like you do. It's somehow easier than turning everything off. Even out here, we often find ourselves living by the clock, though we gave up wearing wristwatches long ago. Time-based days have been hard-wired into our psychological DNA.

Think how pervasive the whole system is. We got used to time before we went to school. TV programs were half an hour long, with commercials every few minutes. Then we went to school and had to be there by 7:21. Not 7:20 or 7:25, but 7:21. Classes were exactly 47 minutes long.

When we went to work, we punched in at a time clock and worked at a job that paid us to produce so many pieces of work at exactly the same time every day, having worked exactly eight hours, no more (or we got overtime) and no less (or they docked our pay).

We had times to get up, times to eat, times to watch television, and times to go to bed. Even the church services I used to lead were designed around the profound spiritual question, "How much stuff can we fit into one hour?" Modern religion deals with metaphysical stuff like that. The clocks in the Sanctuary were usually located in the back, where only the preacher could see them.

And then, when we finally reached 65 and retired from the rat race of time, what did they give us? Ha! A watch!

Finding Stillness / Staying Grounded

I mention all this to make a point. Meditation is hard. Its purpose is to find stillness, timelessness, and peace, a search that is always upstream against the cultural current. Staying grounded and focused doesn't come easily. But if we are ever going to escape the tyranny of the five senses, it's mandatory.

As you continue the meditative practice we began in the last chapter, you'll soon find three areas in which you'll need to concentrate if you want to remain grounded. I call them the heart, the mind, and the body.

1. Be Still, My Heart

My use of the word "heart" here may be confusing. I'm not talking about the beating organ that pumps blood through your veins. I'm referring to your soul, your essence, your very being. When you start to meditate you're usually wound up pretty tightly. You need to relax not just your muscles and pulse rate, but the ineffable sense of "you." Your whole vibration rate, whether you understand that as physical, mental, or psychological, needs to slow down and attune itself to new realities.

The CD I listen to takes about 25 minutes to play through. I always set it to repeat because it usually takes at least that long to find the stillness necessary to engage an OBE. I'm constantly amazed how often it works that way. I have almost come to the point where I expect it. The first time through takes away performance pressure. I'm in no hurry, so I can finally allow myself the luxury of fighting through the jumbled ideas and thoughts that run together at first. I just let them happen. I'm fully committed, leave myself plenty of time, and relax into the stream of things. Only then do things begin to happen.

Here's an example of what I mean:

September 1, 2012

August closed with a bang. Last night at about 8:00 I sat down to meditate. I had the feeling all afternoon that something wanted to get through. As usual, I chalked it up to imagination. But when I sat down and turned on some meditation music I almost immediately felt that I was standing outside my body, looking at myself in the chair.

I decided to remain calm and go with it, but things happened very fast. Even as I thought that I must be somehow playing a mind game with myself, I decided to try to move away from my body, so I affirmed that I was outside on the front porch. There I saw a mental picture of red, orange, and yellow lights flowing out from our Medicine Wheel. In an instant I was there, soaking it in, bringing the light into my body.

The thought suddenly appeared in my head that I was going to make a trip upward, towards the source of the vortex of energy surrounding me.

Then I start to move upward. I'm excited about what I'm going to see and try to imagine all the possibilities, a world of light, a green field, water—all of that—but finally decide to calm down and just wait. I'm looking to stay grounded in peace and stillness.

For a moment I'm aware of my body feeling very light and full of tingling sensations. Then I try to focus, saying "Lead me where I need to go. Teach me what I want to know." My every effort is to remain calm.

Again I have the sense of being drawn upward. Then comes the surprise. I hear my physical voice, later confirmed by Barb, who heard it from the next room, saying, "It's music!"

I don't have the words to express the visual sensation, but it felt like being inside music. I hear a voice saying, aloud, "Stay in the music." But even though I really want to stay, I hear myself saying, "I can't." (Barb heard all this from the next room.)

Immediately I am back in my body, feeling like a failure. What is this compulsion to return home that marks every single trip or adventure I have ever undertaken? Why am I so anxious for every bike trip or hike to end? And now this?

I had nothing more pressing to do. There was nothing I had to accomplish. I wanted, more than anything, to stay and explore. But I felt, for some reason, that I had to come home. I was terribly depressed and angry with myself. Something in me seems to be always thinking about what comes next, rather than what's happening now.

So I just gave up and went to bed.

My impressions, now that a good night's sleep is behind me:

- I am fully aware that I might be doing nothing more than practicing self-hypnosis, for lack of a better word. The reason I feel this way is because all the action seems to be taking place within my head. But my argument for that is simple. Where else can conscious thought take place other than in my head? If I'm going to use words to describe it or attempt to communicate during these episodes, of course it's going to feel like it's in my head!

- The action, when it happens, often takes unexpected twists. If I was going to fool myself, I would think I would follow expected paths and images I've previously read about. This isn't like that. I never seem to know what's going to happen next, and when it does happen, I'm surprised. Take, for example, my words, "It's music!" I've read a lot of OBE accounts, and they are all about familiar imagery of green fields, etc. I've never read about someone being inside music. But this is the second time (the first was some time ago) that I had that experience.

- Speaking of music—it occurred to me that since music is vibration, I might actually have been entering a change in vibrational density. In other words, I could have passed through the field separating this dimension and the next, vibrating at a higher frequency. My subconscious, of course, would have interpreted that and expressed it in the most familiar way—music. It stands to reason that we are correct when we hypothesize that the Medicine Wheel comprises a vortex that connects this dimension to another. It could very well be a "black hole" or "wormhole," for lack of a better word. Energy, perhaps creative energy but certainly sustaining energy, flows through this opening. The dimension on the other side vibrates at a higher frequency, so in order to express that truth, my subconscious had to use the most familiar vibration metaphor it had available—music.

This is an example of what I mean when I say we need to slow down our hearts.

2. Be Still, My Mind

With practice, you can learn to slow down your heartbeat, lower your blood pressure, and calm down. Next to controlling your mind, however, that's child's play. During meditation, the mind is probably the single most difficult thing to deal with.

There are all kind of techniques for this. Some instructors teach students to concentrate on their breathing. Others use monotonous drumming, an age-old technique used by shamans for thousands of years. I've had some success concentrating on a point about two inches in front of my forehead, the place of the Hindu "third eye."

Often a mantra of some kind is recommended. That's just a word or phrase repeated over and over again in order to keep the mind focused and centered. I often use the words I related in the previous account, "Lead me where I need to go. Teach me what I want to know." Sometimes it even works.

Ultimately, however, unless you're a world-class guru, controlling your mind is a futile pursuit. The only thing that reliably works for me is to mentally step out of my body and become what Eckhart Tolle calls "The Watcher." In effect, I've learned (usually) to step away and visualize my body as the guy in the chair, struggling with his mind. I just let him go. It's no longer my fight. Let him deal with it. Once out, I'm free to open the eyes of my essence to whatever possibilities await.

Here's an example from my OBE journal. It covers the process pretty well:

February 18, 2014

I awoke and decided to meditate in bed for a while. I've been frustrated for months now because I can't seem to "break through" to other realities. They're so close that it should be easy once I recognize their existence. But I can't seem to do it. My "monkey brain" takes over and chatters so loud and fast I can't settle in. I've been feeling guilty for this somehow—inadequate— like it's my fault. This morning I tried again to figure it out. My thinking went like this:

I've tried to visualize a place and then go there in my mind. That didn't work. I've tried to empty my mind and be still. That didn't work either. What else can I do? (Now I'm getting angry.) Okay, let's get it on! Face up to the anger. Face up to the guilt. Stop accepting the blame! If mind activity is an adversary, it's a by-product of life in this dimension. I didn't make the rules. It's not my fault!

Suddenly I felt movement—a sideways falling off. Recognizing it, while still angry, I went with it. I had a mental picture of standing outside some kind of building—an abandoned store, as I remember it—and sinking into the concrete sidewalk in front of it. I was up to my knees in cement and should have been afraid. But I was just mad. All I could say was, "Bring it on!"

I sank lower and lower, and welcomed it. Finally I was completely buried in the ground. I felt as though all my guilt, all my anger, all my frustration was encapsulated in my body and buried deep below the earth. But somehow I was completely unafraid because I knew that I could leave this body whenever I wanted. All the bad stuff was being left behind, dead and buried. I felt that this was a metaphor for life.

When we "dive into" this physical dimension from our "Home," the Source, we take on all the material baggage, all the guilt and fear, all the stupid acts of childhood and immaturity, all the "stuff." It's not our fault if we don't overcome it all. It's part of life. It's why we came. Far from being something to be ashamed of, it's the purpose of our life here. From the earliest evolved life-form to the present, it's part of this package called "life experience." Far from being ashamed of it, we ought to revel in it—all the wars, all the dark years of history, all the good times, all the bright moments—they are all part of life. I felt, rather than knew, that this was all as it is supposed to be. The words rang in my mind—it just doesn't matter!

Then came the best part. I had a picture in my mind of my body, containing all the sins, fears, and failures of humankind, buried in the "earth" of material existence, but from this "seed" a flower began to grow. Pure white shoots broke through to a surface in a different dimension. Kindly beings were standing around, watching it grow, interested in its development and nurture. They seemed as though they appreciated the struggle it was going through to produce such a beautiful, pure white stalk. All I could think of was that what we call "life" consists of diving into material existence and "burying ourselves" for a while. Like new life everywhere, it takes the death of a seed to produce a beautiful flower.

And somewhere, somehow, someone appreciates the effort.

How can you experience your own death and burial and not be afraid in the least? Indeed, even welcome it? I haven't the faintest idea. But it happened. It was not at all a fearful vision. It was comforting.

For what seems like a long while I just lay on the bed and luxuriated in what appeared to be the answer to life's great question—"What is the purpose of all this?"

I luxuriated for a while in being "dead." I reveled in all that I had done that I was previously ashamed of—all the lack of effort, all the ego, all the posturing, all the hypocrisy of a public figure who was doing much of it for wrong, selfish reasons. It seemed as though the feelings that brought me the most guilt and shame were exactly the feelings I had come into this life to experience.

As "sick" as that sounds, at the time of the vision it seemed perfectly natural. The "beings" who watched my emergence into a new dimension seemed to appreciate the effort. "Someone has to do it! Thank you!"

There's an old Irish saying: "Is this a private fight or can anybody join in?" Life is like that. It's a fight, a struggle, and has been since the first one-celled organism drew breath, or whatever one-celled organisms do. The past is past. What's done is done. And it had purpose.

The gurus are right: Embrace it all. The Christian theologians are right: Die to self and resurrect to new life.

I hope I can somehow hold on to this!

Alas, it doesn't always work as neatly as it did that time. I fail to still my mind as often as I succeed. Maybe even more often. It's a constant struggle. And the more we struggle, the more difficult it becomes.

The Zen Buddhists are right. We must constantly strive.

And how do we accomplish that?

By not striving!

My advice is to keep working at it. If you find something that works for you, go with it. You'll be glad you did.

3. Be Still, My Body

We come now to the last major hurdle to achieving the necessary peace and stillness needed to engage an OBE. More and more, as you seek to be grounded through meditation, you will learn that your body carries tremendous tensions, reflecting the anxiety of living in the 21st century. Our bodies really *are* connected to our minds. We've known this for a long time, of course. Our language reveals a lot about that knowledge:

He's carrying the weight of the world on his shoulders!

Time has weighed her down!

He has a heavy heart.

She's just worried sick!

And that's just a quick sample.

We can't expect to take on a sped-up, modern cultural system every day and then turn it off at will just because it's time to meditate. That would be too great a burden for the most experienced guru. It takes time. Don't be hard on yourself. It's not your fault.

Have you ever wondered why so many people give cute names to the evening cocktail hour, such as "attitude adjustment time" or "happy hour?" Many people indulge in alcohol, a depressant, to slow them down at the end of a hectic day.

"I need a drink!" they say.

And what's another name for alcohol? Spirits!

That, above all, reveals that people are seeking a spiritual solution as much as a chemical one to the rigors of the day.

By no means am I suggesting that a drink is good for your meditation life. Sometimes it might be. But usually it probably hinders, rather than helps, deep, soul-soothing stillness.

Some people turn to aerobic activity such as walking, running, swimming, or biking. That's what I used to do. But while engaged in my evening run I rarely met smiling runners. They were a pretty serious lot.

So there's no question that such activities point out a basic problem: We are a driven society that needs to find ways to promote stillness rather than over-achievement. I often wonder if meditation should be taught as a basic part of elementary school education. Maybe it would eliminate the need for the numerous medications used to treat attention deficit disorders.

This raises an interesting problem. If, like me, you tend to meditate while lying down, it's really easy to find yourself fast asleep before you achieve an OBE. It's a very common problem. We are, after all, a sleep-deprived, clock-driven culture.

For that reason, most instructors will teach their students to sit, rather than lie down, while meditating. It's hard to fall asleep while sitting up.

But for me, it's also hard to engage an OBE unless I'm lying down. You'll have to experiment on your own to figure out what works best for you.

Here's your objective, though. Bob Monroe called it *Mind Awake / Body Asleep.* You want to be physically relaxed. During an OBE, almost any thoughts related to your body will bring you back right away. That's why it's so important to be comfortable and, as much as possible, stress free. If your back hurts or you develop a pain in your shoulder you will almost certainly find yourself snapped right back to your body.

For me, that means lying prone on my back, in a comfortable, tilt-back, well-padded recliner. If I try to meditate on my side I'll fall asleep every time. If I sit up, my back starts to tighten up.

But that's just me. You may get better results doing something different, especially if you are already experienced in meditation. Experiment!

You also need to eliminate distractions, such as ringing telephones or traffic noises from outside your open window.

Here's where headphones and meditation music really help. It also helps to find a time during the day when you are relaxed but not sleepy, as carefree as possible and not rushed in any way. This is a lot harder than it seems, as you will soon discover. Such times have to be planned and placed on a priority list. They rarely happen by accident.

I've had people say to me, "That's fine for you. You're retired and can plan your own day!"

Well, that's true. But give me a break. There has to be some upside to getting old. When I was working full-time it was a lot more difficult. I'm really sorry not to be able to offer a lot of help here, but that's just the way life is. Our society places a tremendous burden on those who seek an inner spiritual life. It's not easy. But I've come to believe it's worth the effort.

Can you get up to meditate at 3:00 in the morning and still be rested enough to get to work by 8:00? Probably not. But I'll bet you can find a way to fit your schedule around a daily meditation time if it's important enough to you. If not, maybe you need to reconsider your priorities.

Trust me. It's that important!

Summary

We've now begun to develop a systematic approach to engaging an Out-of-Body Experience:

- Make the Decision
- Stick To It
- Develop a System
- Focus, Focus, Focus!
- Stay Calm
- Keep a Journal

To that we now add the following:

Your goal is to achieve a state in which your body is at rest but your mind remains fully engaged. This means finding:

- Stillness of heart
- Stillness of mind
- Stillness of body

Although this takes a lot of practice and is an on-going task that is never really mastered, it is sufficient for now. An OBE won't occur every time. Weeks may go by when nothing happens. But just when you're getting discouraged and thinking about quitting, you will get out of your body. When it *does* happen, you will instantly recognize it as a unique experience. I promise. I don't know how many days or weeks will go by before you find success. To a great extent, that's up to you. But if you are willing to commit at least 30 minutes a day for at least 30 days in a row, I guarantee it will happen. And when it does, it will change your life.

Having experienced your first OBE, you will be ready for some advanced exploration. That's where we'll go next.

EIGHT
ADVANCED EXPLORATIONS

The stream of knowledge is heading toward a non-mechanical reality:
the universe begins to look more like a great thought than like a great machine.
Mind no longer appears to be an accidental intruder into the realm
of matter ... Get over it, and accept the inarguable conclusion.
Sir James Jeans in *The Mysterious Universe*

An Average Writer

For many years I stepped up into a pulpit every week, usually twice each Sunday morning, to face a congregation that spanned a great expanse of spiritual, philosophical, educational, and emotional positions. The names and faces changed, of course, but it was always the same.

On my left sat a typical parishioner, I'll call him Fred, who was very biblically literate. He wanted to hear from someone who studied the New Testament in Greek and the Old Testament in Hebrew and Aramaic, the original languages in which those documents were written. When I made a point, using a specific biblical text, he was interested in the exact meaning of the words; who translated them, how they fit together, and what sources I was citing. He cared about historical context and expected to hear a variety of differing opinions. He wasn't particularly interested in what I thought. He wanted to know what Martin Luther or John Calvin thought. He didn't care about my opinion unless it was shaped by Aristotle or Augustine. He was interested only in exegetical preaching, which is a fancy word that pertains to a method of employing an interpretation based on the exact meaning of the author's words within a framework of historical context.

To my right sat a woman I'll call Sally. She didn't give a hoot about historical accuracy. Her husband had just walked out the door, leaving her with two young kids and no job. She didn't want to hear *about* God, she needed to *feel* a divine presence. Academic word-games were useless to her. She just needed help getting through the day. She wouldn't have recognized an epistemological argument if it came up and bit her on the foot, and didn't know the difference between eschatology and a Labrador retriever. She was there for spiritual underpinning that would help her cope.

Between Fred and Sally sat the rest of the congregation. Each person there occupied a point somewhere on a scale that ran from one extreme to the other. How could I possibly preach a sermon that would satisfy everybody? Neither Fred nor Sally was "wrong." Neither was "right." Both wanted something or they wouldn't have forsaken their comfortable homes, a good cup of coffee, and the Sunday paper in order to come to church. And both were important. If I went too overboard on the academic stuff, Sally would leave without her needs being met. If I erred on the side of practical encouragement, Fred would consider me "sappy" or, even worse, "maudlin." But if I ignored them and preached to the majority in the middle, both would be excluded.

Sad to say, that's what I probably did nine times out of ten. On that basis, you might say I was an "average" preacher. I preached to the average folks—the ones in the middle. Just enough academic stuff to impress the intellectuals, just enough practical stuff to supply the needy. I was Goldilocks in clerical garb.

To some extent I find myself in much the same place as I write this book. You've stayed with me so far and I appreciate it. Maybe you've engaged an OBE by now. Maybe you're still gathering information before you take the plunge.

Some of you "Freds" probably need more scientific evidence. You want to hear about Einstein/Rosenberg bridges, Kruskal's Black Hole Map, curved space, and warped time. You want to study the latest theoretical evidence that proves we live in a Multiverse.

The "Sallys" out there couldn't care less about such things. If even Einstein couldn't get his mind around curved space/time how are *we* going to possibly understand the subject? You're waiting for the examples. You need personal testimonies, not exegetical lectures.

To make matters even worse, the book you now hold in your hands didn't appear there as if by magic. It, too, was guided toward the middle every step of the way. The subject matter was approved by a publisher who needs to sell books if he or she is going to feed their families. No matter how much they love literature it's still a job as much as a calling. For that reason, they need to offer material that appeals to a broad spectrum of people.

But not everyone buys books. So the previous statement has to be modified a bit. The books selected for publication need to appeal to a spectrum of people *who usually buy books.* That thins it down a bit. And that market is reduced further when we consider that we currently live in a very divided world. Every basic demographic is now divided between left and right, conservative and liberal, Democrat or Republican, religious or nonreligious, and etc., and etc. So we have to be very careful about how things are worded so as not to offend anyone who might not buy the book in the first place or, even worse, read it and then use what can, these days, be a mighty big social network to pan it.

When the book finally gets published it goes to book stores and Internet sales companies who want a punchy, marketable title and a catchy cover, as well as a recognizable, preferably one-word, subject under which to advertise it. Is it self-help, how-to-do-it, metaphysical, scientific, religious, paranormal, historical, or what have you? A constant lament of the diminishing number of bookstore owners is, "What shelf do I put it on?"

Please understand. There's nothing wrong with any of this. It's just the way things are. That's life. It works that way not just in the field of literature, but in entertainment, music, religion, politics, sales, science, education, and every other field you can think of. No matter how much we try to hide it, when it comes to business, Goldilocks rules. We usually have to aim for the middle if we want to pay the bills.

That's what this book is going to have to do. If you want pure science, you'll be disappointed. If you're heavy into anecdotal experience, you'll go away unsatisfied.

Call me Goldilocks—the "average" writer.

That being said, though, this chapter will have to slant toward anecdotal examples because there currently exist no microscopes, particle accelerators, mathematical systems, or measuring devices that can possibly view life outside the reality they were designed to observe. They can help us speculate about it, but they can't see it. For that, we need out-of-body travel.

But that becomes subjective and personal really quickly.

I use the term "advanced" explorations for this chapter title because by now you've hopefully had, or soon will have, an initial OBE. That's almost guaranteed to leave you wanting more.

A Highlighted Caution

First, though, I need to issue again a warning that I brought up in the chapter called *First Explorations.*

It's so important I'm going to stress it:

Once you have engaged in a successful Out-of-Body Experience, you will undoubtedly try to reproduce it during your next attempt. This is a trap. Don't do it!

Humans tend to try to build on success. This is a natural and usually efficient way to grow. So if you experience an out-of-body trip that was effective, enjoyable, and productive, it's understandable if you say to yourself, "That's how it's done. I'll just do it again!"

Here's the problem. When you're tip-toeing through the tulips of the Quantum Akashic Field, there are an infinite amount of pathways available to you. To concentrate on only one is to eliminate the possibility of all the others. This is counter-productive and limiting.

Remember the basics. You are shooting for stillness and serenity. That's your responsibility. If you can approach such a state, it opens the doors for those on the other side to meet you, greet you, and help you along.

Think about it this way. If you're visiting a foreign country that practices totally unfamiliar customs and languages, doesn't it just make sense to allow a local who is at home in that country to be your guide? So *your* job is to make yourself available. *Their* job is to guide you where you need to go and teach you what you want to know. Trust them! The universe *wants* to help you. Let it!

Spirit Help

This brings us back to the controversial topic of spirit guides and helpers. In an earlier chapter we talked about the possibility of their existence and speculated about the forms they take. Now we need to go a little further and get specific.

What do spirit guides look like and what can you expect to find?

I've come to believe that the answer is up to you.

Let me explain.

Earlier, when we discussed the *Observer Effect,* we noted that when it comes to quantum reality we tend to find what we are looking for in the form we are expecting to find it. Look for a wave and that's what you'll see. Search for a particle and you'll find one. The observer is intimately connected with that which is being observed. That which the scientist seeks is dependent upon a particular physicist and his or her chosen measuring device to collapse a specific objective into material shape and form.

I think the same principle applies here. I'm not claiming to have cornered the market on truth. But it seems to me, after years of thought, personal experience, research, reading, and study, that seekers who encounter spirit guides tend to visualize them in forms that fit their own background and personal experience.

People who live close to nature usually report seeing animal envoys. Religious folk tend to meet up with angels and other heavenly beings. Technically savvy, sci-fi types are visited by aliens from outer space or other dimensions. Those with Celtic leanings see fairies and leprechauns. Shamans from Peru visit jungle environments. Native Americans travel to mountains and deserts that are familiar to their traditional surroundings. City-folk visualize parks and mowed grass.

On and on it goes. Which of these pictures is correct?

All of them! And none of them!

The landscapes I have just described are called *Consensus Realities*. The theory behind their existence is that when a large group of people, over many years, focuses on a specific reality, they bring it into existence and tend to "harden" it, so to speak, into a palpable, if spiritual, reality.

The Christian concept of Heaven is no doubt such a Consensus Reality, as are Jewish and Muslim descriptions of the afterlife. When enough people, for a long enough time, firmly believe and carefully describe such a reality, that's what their followers expect to find. Then of course, they find it.

It's an idea that forms the basis of an old joke stemming from Jesus's words, "In [God's] house are many mansions."

When a newcomer is first being escorted through Heaven, he passes closed room after closed room.

"Who's in there?" he asks his guide.

"Shhhh!" says the guide. "They think they're the only ones here!"

The truth, to me, seems to be that we probably can't picture what reality really looks like. Let's go back to the idea of language again. I've said it before, but it bears repeating: *Language is a human invention designed to describe things that exist in our material perception realm as interpreted by our senses.* Once we move outside that reality, language is useless. We can't say, "This is what it *is*!" All we can say is, "This is what it's *like*!"

And language changes as cultures evolve. I find it fascinating, for instance, that the opening chapters of Genesis, the first book of the Bible, describes paradise as a forest-like garden of Eden. Sixty-six books later, in Revelation, the Bible's final book, paradise is described as a magnificent city.

What happened in between those two descriptions?

Civilization happened! Paradise didn't change. People did.

All this is to say that I can't tell you what your spirit guides will look like.

All I can relate is how they appear to me, and hope that will help prepare you to engage your own experiences in your own way, given your own background and culture.

Animal Envoys

Because I live in the woods and am constantly surrounded by animal energy, it seems natural to me that after a dream or OBE my brain will remember animal imagery when it comes to write about what happened.

Let me give you some examples from my OBE journal:

January 13, 2014

I felt very frustrated this morning. For some time now I haven't been able to get out of body or experience anything that resembles a real shamanic journey. Spiritually, I'm feeling out of touch. I'm probably trying too hard, but I don't know what to do about it.

In this frame of mind I took our dog Rocky for an early morning walk in the wet, cold woods.

At the Shaman's Circle I was moved to stop and confess my sins. I'm finally beginning to understand a lot about why I did things that I'm not proud of—indeed, ashamed of. I am now, at my maturing age, fully aware of my mistakes.

With this accomplished I had a strong sense that a group of spirit beings were surrounding and supporting me. I was moved to go to the center of the circle. I felt as though this will someday be my place—that I will be the teaching elder of the circle, replacing Grandfather, the current spirit guide/ teaching elder who will rise to a new level of service on a yet higher plain. I hope that's not just my ego talking.

It was an encouraging feeling, and on its own would have been sufficient to call the morning a success. But there was more to come.

Rocky and I walked to the gazebo and went in to meditate. Immediately I had the feeling of doing a forward dive down the hill and into a cave buried below the Medicine Wheel. I've been there before. It's a powerful place of shamanic magic. It's very dark but somehow comforting at the same time. It's not at all frightening.

There in the cave, Panther came to me. He just sat and stared at me. I felt as though he was giving me a message, but I didn't yet know what it was. What I did understand was that my current state of emotional frustration was akin to being in a spiritual cave. There is nothing to do but wait. All will happen in its proper time.

Later I looked up the message of Panther in Ted Andrews's *Animal Speak*:

"Astral travel—Guardian energy—Symbol of the feminine
Understanding of death—Reclaiming one's power
Ability to know the dark—Death and rebirth

The panther marks a new turn in the heroic path of those to whom it comes. It reflects a reclaiming of that which was lost and an intimate connection with the great archetypal force behind it. It gives an ability to go beyond what has been imagined."

September 1, 2014

I learned about the meaning of acceptance this morning. As always, the lesson was totally unexpected and completely different than I thought it would be. As seems to be the case these days, it was followed by the unexpected sight of an unexpected animal on a subsequent hike or bike ride.

A few weeks ago, during an OBE, I was visited by Hummingbird. It flew so close to my face that I flinched, thereby forcing an abrupt return to my body. As I sat at the computer to write about the experience I glanced out the window and saw a hummingbird stuck on the front porch. To me, Hummingbird has always signified renewal. I immediately got up and opened the screen doors so it could fly away to freedom.

During my meditation on August 20th, Fox appeared, telling me that magic is afoot. That very day I spotted a fox on my morning bike ride. It just sat by the side of the road, waiting for me to almost pull up alongside him. Then he quietly jumped into the woods and disappeared.

While meditating on August 22nd, Coyote said to balance wisdom and fun in my endeavors—to trust that all is happening according to plan and to do what is best, even if it is difficult. For the next few weeks, we found coyote droppings all over our network of woods trails. In typical trickster fashion, they left us signs without letting us see them.

This morning, the biggest "V" of geese I've seen in a long time crossed the road right in front of me on my morning bike ride. It happened exactly as the full meaning of today's OBE lesson dropped into place. What was the message? To heed the call to a new quest; to be open to new wonders and possibilities; to pursue new adventures and explore new travels.

In light of all this, all I could do was laugh with joy.

Classroom Aid

My guides are not always animals, however. I've spent a lot of time teaching in public schools, colleges, and churches. I've attended a lot of classes. So sometimes my trips take the form of an educational experience:

December 16, 2014: The Meaning of Life—A Teaching

Unable to nap during a busy day of carpentry, I lay down to meditate, expecting to fall asleep. It's been a long season of frustration. I haven't been able to connect very well. I've been too distracted by projects. But immediately upon starting some meditation music I seemed to physically dissolve, leaving only my non-material self, my essence, freed from my body. I felt myself drawn to an old stone circle, the first one that we excavated and restored and the one nearest to our house. Recently we discovered, through dowsing, that it was the oldest sacred circle on our property. It was the place where I first met Sobuko and learned his name. There we discovered that he was the first shaman who lived and worked here, at least 25,000 years ago.

Sobuko was there waiting for me and took me immediately to the Shaman's Circle on the hill. There, after I joined the circle, Grandfather, the teaching elder, sat in his accustomed place to teach us.

This story may not be word-for-word correct. But it's very close. I wrote it down as soon as I returned to my body…

The lesson today is about the meaning of life.

A rich man entered a village and offered a reward to anyone who could reveal to him the meaning of life.

A prominent teacher came forward and said, "The meaning of life is found in love."

"That may be so," said the rich man, "but I cannot make myself love what I consider to be unlovable. The best I can do is pretend to feel what I do not feel. Surely the meaning of life cannot be found in falsehood."

And he dismissed the prominent teacher.

A successful businessman then stepped forward.

"The meaning of life," he said, "is to be found in activity. Busy people are successful people, and successful people are happy."

"But I find happiness in leisure as well," said the rich man. "Surely the meaning of life is not to be found only in the things that lead to happiness, for many happy people know deep down that they live meaningless lives."

And the businessman walked away.

Then a poor man stepped forward. He was a beggar and despised by all.

"The meaning of life," he said, "is found in the knowledge of the certainty of death."

"Explain," said the rich man.

The poor man continued. "Only when you know that death is imminent, when you know it is at your very doorstep, can you come to really feel the moment you are in right now, for you realize it may be your last experience of life. The present moment becomes crystal clear, sharp, and vivid. And the meaning of life is to be found in fully experiencing the clarity of every living moment. That, after all, is why we choose to be born in the first place."

The poor beggar won the reward. He had revealed the meaning of life.

With a start I came out of my vision. It had been short, but extremely powerful.

August 22, 2015: A Dream and A Message
The Dream

I awoke from a dream at about 1:00. I dreamed I was at a church with which I used to be peripherally connected. The people, some of whom I once knew well, seemed to be performing a play I had supposedly written years before. In the dream, I had forgotten that I had written it, but it was very vivid.

When I woke up I couldn't remember ever having written such a play. But it seemed real at the time.

Of course, the reality is that I've never written a play. It just seemed as if I had. I had to convince myself that the memory was imaginary.

It became obvious that I needed to meditate right away. There were things I just had to know, so I forced myself out of bed and into meditation mode.

Soon after I began, everything became clear. I had written a play and forgotten about it. It was a play called "Life of Jim!" I wrote it before I was born and came to earth to live it. It was in three acts, following a prologue. Each act contained the seed theme of the next act, and each seed was sown at a cabin in the woods, built by my own hands. The overall message of the play was spiritual growth—a search for The Source.

Prologue

I prepared for life over the course of my first 21 years. During that time I learned and acquired the basic skills I would need later on—music, carpentry, public speaking, audience involvement, and confidence.

Act 1: "A"—Religion

During this stage of my life, which lasted about twenty years, the main theme consisted of developing a religion and establishing a base for belief systems while learning to perform on stage and preach. The seeds of Act 2 were sown in the cabin I built in New Hampshire. There I met a nude woman on a rock who upset my current belief structure, forcing me to begin to transform and evolve.

Act 2: "B"—Rejection of Religion

Another twenty-year period. Here the main theme was breaking all the rules from Act 1 and living a pretty worldly life. I searched for the spiritual in pleasure and ego. The seeds for the next act were finally sown at a cabin I built in western Massachusetts. Here I encountered my first animal envoy, a ruffed grouse, near a fallen standing stone that I subsequently raised.

Act 3: "A1"—Spiritual

This stage has lasted, so far, for a little more than a decade. The main theme was a return to a more mature understanding of religion. The next-act seeds, the act that will probably begin with my physical death, were sown at the house I built a few years ago, the place in the woods where I now live.

This was the play I wrote before I began this life, and then promptly forgot, as we all do, once I was born. It was the story of my life. I don't know how long it has to go before the final curtain rings down, but I'm sure its end is near. I hope there's some applause at the end.

I would have been happy to be able to pause and digest all this, but there's more. When I came to realize that my life (all our lives) are a play that we, ourselves, have written, I was still dreaming out of body. I decided to go to the Shaman Circle for counseling.

Once more I was surprised. Those who keep watch there were standing and clapping, welcoming me home and thus fulfilling my hope for applause. They seated me in the middle, the place where grandfather, the teaching elder, usually sat. I was now the teacher. I had a sudden sensation of once again being outside the universe, holding it in my hands. But now it was my cosmos, written and directed by me.

Everything made perfect sense. I was the Source, as are we all. I sat in a circle with some key folks in my life. One of them was an older woman from my extended family whom I have always disliked. I even consider her to be one of the two evil people I have met in my life. Now I learned that she had volunteered to teach me how to hate and forgive. I'll never think of her quite in the same way.

To her I now say thank you. In the next life I'll thank you personally. If I did it now, I doubt you would understand. But it took courage on your part and I appreciate it.

It doesn't end here. I was next conscious of my Astral Body. The colors of the rainbow seemed to be flowing out from my head as I watched. But then I realized that it was actually quite the reverse. They were flowing in, not out. With this insight I understood that I've had it backwards. I wasn't born here, in this body, and then later found my Astral Body. The Astral was created prior to this body. It's been here all along. I've visited it in sleep without understanding what was happening. First came the Astral, then the physical.

Once again the Biblical authors had it right:

Genesis 1: God says, "Let us make man in our image." If we are "God," there appears to be individual consciousness even in the unity of Akasha. We then "created" our physical body. And we are not alone. That's why "God" uses the plural "us."

Genesis 2: "God breathed into (us) the breath of life (life = energy = light). And (we) became a living soul." The Astral body of energy/light/life.

I'm going to work this out further someday, but all in all it's been a very fruitful time. I've found the Source. My life has meaning. As is the case for everyone!

Human-like Guides

The most common identity spirit guides assume, or should I say our most common way of remembering them, is in a guise close to human form.

I've already talked about Sobuko, my friend and guide who I suspect is "me" on the other side—my Higher Self. In my mind he definitely has human form. But others have appeared in this guise to teach me lessons I needed to know. Here's one example:

August 30, 2015
Perhaps the most powerful dream yet—or OBE—or vision?

I was up at the Shaman Circle, facing a cave opening. It was filled with light, streaming down as if it were a waterfall. I walked up to it and tried to go through, but couldn't. I don't know why. I just stood and watched the changing colors and arrays.

Then I seemed to be at a standing stone we erected down near our driveway entrance. Slowly I again made my way up toward the Shaman Circle. But this time the members stood in a straight line between the circle and me, barring me from joining them—barring me from the circle. There was no menace or anger. I didn't feel at all threatened. But they were firm in denying me entrance. The expression on their faces was inscrutable. This whole scene was totally unexpected. I had felt welcomed before, a part of the circle of men. But now they gently, but firmly, were saying "No!" They looked at me with a resolute kindness. "Tough love," perhaps.

Although no one pointed, I felt directed to the Medicine Wheel. Somehow I understood that before I could go any further I needed to learn more about a special aspect of women's strength. On my way there I made a note to remind myself to have Barb teach me more about the plants and flowers she has planted around the place. I thought I needed to be in more intimate touch with Gaia. But I quickly learned that this was not necessarily what I had to learn. So I began to think about women's strength in a different way.

Like most men over the past 50,000 years or so, I associated such strength with the mystery of birth and new life. After all, that's the mystery that has been so ritualized, feared, hemmed in with law, held in awe, and memorialized in myth. But that isn't the main thrust of strength that I had to learn about today.

No, with a blinding, powerful, extremely sad and profound jolt, I came to know in a flash what an aspect of women's strength, only one of the gifts with which women have blessed the world, really is. It is a lesson that can come only through difficult and painful experience—an experience I'm not sure I have the stamina to obtain.

This is the secret that I had to learn—ACCEPTANCE. It came to me in a flash, and made me incredibly sad.

For thousands of years women have been down-graded, held back, denigrated to second-class status, and in some cases degraded. Often men have put them on a pedestal, which was just a lying, false way of putting women in a prison. ("Honey, don't worry your pretty little head about voting. You have more important things to do." Yeah. Right!) Through that incredibly long and painful process, women have been forced to learn the lesson of how to survive and continue on—Acceptance.

That doesn't mean resignation. It doesn't mean hopelessness. It doesn't mean weakness. It means hope through strength, accepting what is, and never giving up. Perseverance. Think, for instance, of the plight of an African American woman living the black experience over the last 300 years. Taken from her family and tribe, treated as both forced labor and breeder of new slaves, then obtaining "freedom" only to have her husband, in so many cases, either be murdered in brave rebellion, discriminated against by a white society, or absent through an inability to cope. She is left to raise the family, to carry on, to keep hope alive by resigning herself to never give up. This is a lesson that most men will simply never understand. This is hope in action. "Maybe I can't change things alone, but I can carry on so that my children can try!"

It is the cry of the woman who does work equal to that of a man but is forced to accept a lower wage. It is the plea of a woman patronized by the "good old boy" network—the "little lady back home." The one who has to take care of the kids while her man is off having fun and complaining to his male companions about how difficult life is. The one to whom vacation means doing the same things she has to do back home but in more primitive conditions.

Women's strength is acceptance of what is while never losing the vision of the way things should be. It's not Feminism, as important as that is. Feminism is too often simply the art of women learning to take power as men have traditionally done, or learning to beat men at their own game. This is a necessary swing of the pendulum, but it's not the kind of strength I needed to learn now. Not even close.

Women have a strength most men will never understand. It's been bought at a tremendous price—thousands of years of suffering and fighting within a patriarchal system. But the great cost has bought a great treasure—a pearl of great price—the gift of Acceptance.

Most men will never obtain it. They don't have the strength to pay the price. But this seems to be what I am being asked to do—what I must do if I am going to progress.

I've always been a "doer." Mostly, both domestically and in my work, I have felt a patriarchal obligation to pull women along with me. The church is disproportionately populated by women despite being run by men, and I have been surrounded by feminine energy. But I have learned to manipulate that energy to get things done, and, in the process, forwarded my own agenda. It wasn't done out of maliciousness. To my shame, it was done out of ignorance.

It now appears that I have a great lesson to learn before I can rejoin the Circle of Shamans. They have excluded me until I learn Acceptance. I guess that means spending more time at the Medicine Wheel, a place of specific feminine energy. Where this will lead is anyone's guess. Only time will tell. But I'm scared stiff. I'm not sure I have the strength to completely relearn and change what I am. But not to do so probably means I will be destined to live many more lives until I do.

"Teach me what I need to know." I don't know if I'm ready, or how to proceed. But I must.

Summing It All Up

I could go on and on with examples such as this. I have a notebook full of them. I write about them not to say this is what you should expect when you have an OBE, however, but rather to point out the endless variety of experiences you can expect. Each one of us is living our own story. We all stand at different viewing platforms, based on what we have experienced so far in life. Whatever appears to you, it will undoubtedly be somewhat unique. That's what you should work with. That's what *you* need to know. That's what the cosmos is trying to tell *you*.

Once again, let's return to basics. First, the overall plan:
- Make the Decision
- Stick To It
- Develop a System
- Focus, Focus, Focus!
- Stay Calm
- Keep a Journal

Then you need to proceed. In order to outflank your senses, which are used to dealing with a pretty frantic pace of life, you need to seek:
- Stillness of heart
- Stillness of mind
- Stillness of body

Although you won't achieve perfection, if you meditate for at least 30 minutes a day for at least thirty days, you will undoubtedly succeed in moving at least part-way away from your body. When you do, you'll know it. Afterwards you may doubt it and chalk the whole experience up to imagination, but in your heart you'll know you've done it. That will leave you wanting more. You'll be able to move into advanced exploration.

For that you'll need a guide—a native of the new country you've visited. So here's the next step:

- Spirit guides come in an almost infinite variety of forms.
- The form you encounter will be a form you will recognize, based on your past experience. In other words, your brain will sort through your personal "rolodex" of experiences and choose to explain what is basically unexplainable by selecting a form you can most easily identify and feel comfortable with.
- Remember that your spirit guides probably don't really look like the way they appear to you. It's only an approximation. But that's not important. It's about the message, not the messenger. Trust it!

At this point my advice is to again stop, settle down, and spend some time putting all this into practice. You have lessons to learn that no one can teach you except the guides you meet.

To put it bluntly, what I'm saying is that from here on in, you're on your own. You are about to experience something that no one can prepare you for. If you experience a little fear, that's understandable. The unknown always produces some trepidation.

But remember that love is a constant throughout the universe. That's not just a cliché, either. The universe *wants* you to succeed. The arc of evolution is always upward. The process moves slowly, but if you look back over a few thousand years of our species' growth, a few hundred years of cultural gains, or even a few dozen years of personal development, love and compassion grind slowly, if exceedingly small.

This stage of your OBE development will vary considerably from person to person. Some people experience one out-of-body trip and it lasts them a lifetime. Others want to return again and again. Your experience will be unique to you.

But if you decide to continue, from time to time you'll want to evaluate why you are doing this. Is it for spiritual growth? Do you want to seek answers to questions you have about the purpose and meaning of your life? Are you looking for a healing—ether spiritual or physical? Is it simply curiosity? Are you hoping to alleviate the fear of death?

All those are legitimate questions, and although I can't answer them in a way that will completely satisfy you, I can make some predictions based on my own experience.

1. You will feel an immense and continual relief that you are immortal, that you are part of a much larger reality than you previously thought, that you need not fear death, and that life as you now know it is precious and awesome.

2. You will come to understand that even though you don't have all the answers to your philosophical questions, the answers are available in this life and you now know how to go about finding them.

3. You will probably have a greater retention of dreams and visions. This is a two-sided coin, however. There are some dreams you probably won't want to remember. Life is sometimes pretty confusing.

4. You might develop a greater sense of patience when it comes to observing how people live in this world, both in the public arena and in your private circles. I haven't yet. But you might! Increased patience is often reported by those who have OBEs.

5. You will undoubtedly develop a better self-image and display more confidence in the choices you make. This comes about when you come to know in your heart as well as in your head that you have unseen help throughout life.

6. You might be able to explore the whole idea of past-life regression while coming to understand why you are the way you are. This is called Karma, and it's fascinating!

7. You will probably take comfort in the fact that guides and helpers from other dimensions are only a thought away. For some reason, I don't know why, this seems to be increasingly important as I get older.

8. This may be unique to me, but you may develop, as I have, an aversion to violence. I hunted and fished all my life. When I moved to the woods I expected to eat a lot of wild game. Now I feed the deer, laugh at the squirrels, play with the birds, and get upset over how many TV shows begin with a murder. I'm not a vegetarian, and I still enjoy the wild game my neighbors sometimes supply, but I don't want to shoot anything anymore. I've sold my guns, and my bow and arrows lie dormant in my shed. A few years ago I caught a rabbit in a live trap. He'd been eating my garden. My first thought was—dinner! But I just couldn't do it. I wound up driving him to a field a few miles away and letting him go.

These are a few things you have to look forward to. Enjoy the process. Don't rush it. Revel in it!

When you're ready, we can continue together.

NINE
BACK TO EARTH

If I knew with no trace of doubt what I would be and do after I died,
it would change me radically. I could live my physical life to the fullest.
Robert Monroe in *Ultimate Journey*

A New Beginning

In the first month of the year 2012, early in January, I lost my stability. I had been troubled by epileptic seizures for a few years. They had begun, to the best of my recollection, when I lived in Florida, sometime during the years between 2006 and 2009, probably brought on by stress. But these were also the years I first began to think in terms of vibrational energies separating alternate dimensions.

As I briefly mentioned earlier, Epilepsy has long been thought to be associated with spirituality. The reason for this is that people who have epileptic seizures sometimes experience visions and what are usually called hallucinations. Indeed, MRI studies show that what is often called both the "shamanic experience" and the OBE experience affect the same portion of the brain that is lit up during epileptic seizures.

There was no question in my mind that my seizures happened more often, and were of greater intensity, when I had been visiting the land where we now live in South Carolina. It wasn't *being* there, though, as much as it was *leaving*. I could count on them whenever we drove back to Florida. Even so, after moving up here full time to live on the land, they worsened, culminating in an incident in which I got a speck of wood in my eye while doing some chainsaw work. While Barb drove me to an eye doctor I had the first episodes of what I assume were grand mal seizures—very severe. As they continued during the next year, a few of them were accompanied by impressions of lights, tunnels, and even, once, people of light standing off to one side. I started to do a lot of Internet research.

I was afraid to take meds or even see a doctor. My feeling was, strange and egotistical as it may sound, that there was a good possibility that the seizures were happening for a reason. Because I had started flirting with Out-of-Body Experiences, which are usually accompanied by vibrations, I felt that the seizures might be re-wiring a section of my brain that I, through a lifetime of left-brain, analytical, religious, and theological thought, might have, by habit and misuse, allowed to atrophy.

Now I began to think that this was a shortcoming that needed to be adjusted. Were the seizures my way of opening up the very neurological connections in my brain that I would need in order to be responsive to voices from outside our perception realm? Perhaps they were even caused because energies on this particular piece of land actually altered my vibrational center in some way.

In short, I was afraid that if I chemically closed the door to the "bad guys" of epileptic seizures, I might also be closing the door to the "good guys" of spiritual entities.

That being said, I began to make some allowances. Barb took over most of the driving, and I was very careful. But otherwise I adopted a wait-and-see approach.

For various reasons I had begun to suspect that the year 2012 was going to be, for us at least, a year of change and instability, although I don't think the word "instability" came up until later in the year. With all the Mayan long-count calendar hype about that year, and because I was the co-author of a book about the end of the world (*Armageddon Now: The End of the World A to Z*, written with my wife Barbara) I was obviously wondering if all these omens were real. I kind of believed it, but not really. I was, in other words, willing and ready, but agnostic.

During the second week of January I had a vicious epileptic seizure that knocked me right off my feet. The results of the seizure itself quickly passed, but while it was going on I severely hurt my ankle. Although I never had an X-ray done, I think I must have fractured a bone or two. At the very least I sprained, pulled or tore some ligaments and tendons. As late as August the ankle was still swollen and tender. My other Achilles heel, the left one, was also quite painful. Walking was very difficult. Running and biking were, of course, almost impossible. I was forced to spend months at a time, especially during January and February, off my feet, moving only with a cane or walking stick while wearing ankle braces on both feet.

It had certainly been a year of "instability" in that regard. But the instability manifested itself in many other ways. That was the year I began to develop the material in this book about seeking an OBE experience in a serious and systematic way. Other changes, some quite radical, followed. Many were positive. A few were negative. But it certainly was a year of instability, symbolized by my very unstable ankles. Through most of the year we were unable to feel fully "grounded." The physical condition of unstable ankles was an outward manifestation of a spiritual upheaval occurring in our lives.

Ankles have long been a problem with me. A central core of the message of *Journey Home*, my first book, involved a severe ankle sprain that cut short a bike trip designed to fulfill a spiritual quest. It seems to be a common theme running through my whole life.

But this year of instability ended up being a turning point. A new chapter of our lives was beginning. Up until then we lived not "in" the land but "on" the land. We had been living in a trailer. Quite literally, there was no foundation connecting us to the land. Then, starting in October, we began to build a house on a solid footing, rooted in the land itself.

At first we worried about digging into Gaia and disturbing the soil, but soon viewed the situation quite differently. In short, the year that began with "instability" ended with us being rooted and grounded in Gaia. We weren't violating her. She was receiving us. It's the difference between sex and making love. We had, in short, come back to earth.

There is no such thing as coincidence. Timing is as magical as the event itself. That summer I began to keep a dream and OBE journal. By now you may have noticed that many of the journal entries I have shared in this book were written during 2012. All were written since then.

Take this entry, for instance, written two years after my ankle injury. I've written about it before in my book *Supernatural Gods*, and here use it with the permission of the publisher, Visible Ink Press:

October 14, 2014

I've had some OBEs in the last two weeks but, for some reason, haven't wanted to write about them. Perhaps doubt. Perhaps sloth. Perhaps a nagging fear that my imagination might sometimes run amuck. But there's no imagining what happened today. There is physical proof. In short—I received a healing.

Two of my recent OBEs involved meeting a feminine energy entity that I call Brigit. At first, I thought she was a lost soul. She was standing by a bay of water and looking out to sea. I thought she must be waiting for a lost husband to return from a voyage and I tried to help her move on, but I couldn't get through. The second one revealed the truth. She wasn't lost at all. She is a patron saint of Ireland, "baptized" by the Christian Church to adopt her from her original incarnation as a pagan goddess of women, which is only one of her many duties. I figured that my recent desire to go to Ireland might have inspired this thought, so I was a bit skeptical and didn't follow it up much. But then I saw her again. I began to think that my thoughts of Ireland might have somehow opened a door to her, inviting her to enter my life. Little did I know how important that open door would become.

For the last week I've been on my feet a lot, and a once badly sprained, or perhaps broken, ankle has been giving me nagging problems. For the last three days I've been wearing a brace and using a cane. To say the least, I've been very discouraged.

Today it rained. It's slippery outside. For a third straight day I've been confined inside. To make matters worse, I've been gaining weight again and riding a bike seems out of the question. At my age, that's the only physical activity that helps keep my weight down. On top of that, I've had small epileptic seizures for the past two days, and this morning had a big one.

Around noon I had a strong yen to go down to our gazebo, so I grabbed my cane, picked up a book, and walked out towards the woods. Because I was trying to get away without getting Rocky, our dog and constant companion, all excited I snuck out the back door and, in my hurry, forgot my ankle brace. I didn't want to go back inside, so I decided that even though it was really slippery I'd just be careful. When I got there I sat down and read a little, then tried to meditate.

Within seconds I felt something happening. A moment later I was out of body and standing by the small monument of stones we've built overlooking our Medicine Wheel:

I look down at the Medicine Wheel and see Brigit standing there at the center, welcoming me with open arms. When I went down to greet her I asked if she was an incarnation or manifestation of Gaia. She said she was Gaia's daughter, a manifestation emanating from the Earth Mother. The circle was filled with women engaged in a ritual of some kind. They stood in a ring around the Medicine Wheel, watching me. I suppose I should have been a bit bashful. I was completely naked and obviously a man. But I wasn't uncomfortable at all. Instead, I told Brigit that my ankle was hurt. She immediately knelt down and began to stroke my ankle with both hands. I remember thinking that the problem wasn't in my astral ankle, it was in my real ankle up in the Gazebo. But I didn't say anything because I was aware of a healing touch, a kind of vibration, in my ankle. So I just let it happen.

(I seem to remember here being told that I had to submit if we were to go further. To me, "submit" is a bad word. It has negative connotations. But this feeling wasn't negative at all. There was no hierarchy or ranking involved. It was just a need to let go and permit what was to come. And I did—consciously.)

At any rate, my attention was immediately drawn away from the ankle because I was, in the presence of all the female witnesses, given a crash course in sexuality. Not just sex, although that was involved, but sexuality. I really can't go into all the ins and outs, so to speak, but it became obvious that human sex is merely a crude grasping for something that is spiritually very profound—a search for timeless individuality within unity. I was made instantly aware of why I, and everyone else, has certain things that "turn them on," so to speak. Questions I've had about my early childhood, way before I was sexually active or even capable of it, were answered in explicit detail. Now it all became clear that there was a greater purpose being acted out.

When the lesson was over (there's more, but let's leave it at that!) a strange thing happened. I was placed prone on the ground and somehow kind of "pressed in" to Gaia herself. It wasn't sex, it was a more profound and complete merging with the earth, soil, moss, and drippy, moist things. I was, in short, partially dismembered and buried. But it was very pleasant. I really enjoyed the experience.

When I stood up again, there was Sobuko, my out-of-body friend and spirit guide, walking down the hill and joining us at the Medicine Wheel. He stood in the center with Brigit as they faced each other and joined hands—male and female. One by one the women in the circle would walk to them and stand between their held hands. Sobuko and Brigit would lift their arms and then—whoosh!—the women would shoot up into the air and out of sight. When my time came I could hardly wait. Both Sobuko and Brigit were smiling. It seemed to be a wonderful game. They lowered their arms on both sides of me and then lifted them again. Suddenly I seemed to be transformed into a beam of rainbow-hued light. I shot up into the air and out of the universe, looking down on planets and stars. It was a similar experience to what I've had before, of looking at the universe from above and outside, but I wanted more. I wanted a cleansing. So I flew instantly to the sun in order to burn away all impurities. It was wonderful. I flew right into the sun and enjoyed every second of it.

Immediately, however, I was back in my body in the gazebo. I felt I had just woke up from a powerful dream, half here and half there. I decided to go back to the house and tell Barb about it.

It was only when I was halfway back that I realized I was walking normally, without any pain at all. Even on the slippery ground I began to dance and was sure-footed, without a twinge. I took a short nap and slept like a baby for half an hour, then drove to town and went to the grocery store. No cane and no pain. When I got back to the house and told Barb about the story, I even danced around the living room. Unheard of two hours ago. My ankle was completely healed.

I don't understand what happened, but you don't "imagine" or "dream up" a healing of this sort. This is physically real. All I can do is accept it and say thank you. Which I did. And do!

There it is, for better or for worse. I don't understand it, I wasn't expecting it, and I certainly don't blame anyone who refuses to accept it as anything other than a figment of my fertile imagination. For much of my life that's exactly what I would have believed.

I only know this. I haven't had any problems with my ankle from that date to the present time.

Life is indeed mysterious.

Practical OBEs

If you want to come back to earth by asking if there is any practical reason for seeking to engage an OBE, there it is. You can't get more practical than a physical healing.

Am I saying that you will receive a healing if you need one?

No! I have no idea why spontaneous healings sometimes occur. I'm sure it has nothing to do with some people being more "worthy" than others, or some people having more "faith" than others. All I'm saying is that shamanic practitioners have, for thousands of years, sought healing for their patients. Sometimes, not always, they have been successful, and we simply cannot ignore the evidence.

There are many people, I'm sure, who won't believe OBEs are real because so much evidence seems to be anecdotal. But a physical healing is pretty straightforward. Especially when it happens to you.

I once tried to come up with a way to describe folks who won't accept anything based on the personal experience of someone else. These people need proof of a different kind. They are just like I used to be. Doubters.

Perhaps that's why my favorite disciple in the New Testament has always been the one called "Doubting" Thomas. When the other disciples told him about Jesus' resurrection his response resonated with me: "I'll believe it when I see it!"

Then, as the story goes, he met the risen Christ.

What was his response? "My Lord and my God!"

I guess for much of my life you could have called me "Doubting Jim" when it came to paranormal testimonies.

But now I wonder if such a condition has a different name: Narcissism. Here's how I define it:

Narcissism is believing that only your own experience is sufficient to determine whether or not you believe in something.

It sounds a bit tough on the doubters of the world. But there it is. Narcissists, and remember that I speak from personal experience, believe they and they alone are capable of proving something real. You'll find them all over the Internet these days. I know of no public person who has escaped the scorn of people who know just enough to comment negatively on something or someone, but not enough to understand what they're trying to say. No one, from Deepak Chopra, to Barak Obama, to Magic Johnson, is immune from that kind of ridicule.

To prove my point, all you have to do is listen to sports TV on Monday morning. There's always criticism of some athlete who made a mistake in yesterday's game. Armchair narcissists who have never been athletes are ready and willing to heap scorn on someone for doing something "wrong." They imply, of course, that *they* would never make such a mistake.

The same thing happens to public figures; actors, politicians, scientists, TV personalities, and, dare I say it, writers. Because of the contemporary ascension of social media narcissists, we seem to have more "experts" out there than ever. A lot of people seek a like-minded following. From the comfort of their own homes, communicating only by computer, such people often claim to know best how to run the world. How they would perform if the responsibility actually fell on their shoulders is another matter.

I've endured my share of criticism aimed at articles and books I've written. Sometimes it's deserved, but often it's obvious the critics have no grasp of the subject. It happens to every author I've ever known. The bigger the name, the harsher the criticism.

This is par for the course when it comes to the world of ideas, but once you've experienced an actual physical healing under conditions outside your perception realm, you can't help but come back to earth with a bang. A physical cure is real and beyond subjective opinion. Perceived entities from "beyond" now claim your attention. They want to help. Perhaps they even want to be helped by you. Maybe it's a two-way street. Who knows? Is it possible that they are just as anxious to meet you as you are to meet them? Are they, too, experimenting with inter-dimensional connections? Are they as surprised as you when you connect?

Consider the following:

December 10, 2017

I awoke early this morning, around 4:00, and went out on the back porch to read and meditate.

As I began I had a strong compulsion to forgo my usual *Sleeping Through the Rain* CD, and selected instead, *Music Of Graceful Passages*. It turned out to be a prophetic choice, because my meditation was all about passages.

It came to me, soon after I focused, that perhaps the task I now face is to free the Shamans and Wise Women of the circle and Medicine Wheel. Up until now it had never even occurred to me that they might be here for reasons other than the fact that they wanted to help. But what if they have become so attached to this property and the earthly task they had undertaken, out of loving compassion, that they somehow "tied" themselves to this sphere? What if they needed my help? Do they need to be "danced" to freedom? Is that why I am here?

I was so used to thinking of these entities as all-knowing spirits that it simply never entered my head that they might need me as much as I need them.

All my life I have felt as though I had a task to do that I didn't yet recognize. By now I figured I had somehow missed it. Maybe it was greater success, or fame as a preacher or musician, or some such thing. Now I wonder if this is it.

I once received a message that felt so important I printed it out and hung it on my wall. I've quoted it in two books: "You have come full circle, back to where it all began." Does that mean that Sobuko was the first "me" here, just as I am, perhaps, the last? Is a long circle of Karma finally beginning to close?

If that is the case, and it's time for some of these local entities to leave this plane and continue on, having completed their work here, I'm happy for them. But it makes me sad, as well. I will miss having them around. When they are gone the place will have quite a different feel. But how can I not carry out this task, if that is what drew me here after a lifetime of preparation?

Music and Theology. Vibration and Spirituality. A lifetime of push/pull phobia toward dance. I didn't want to dance myself, but I loved playing in dance bands. That meant, as I wrote earlier, that "dance was so sacred

I could not sully it by reducing it to mere entertainment." My spiritual life began with Grouse telling me to get in touch with the dance of life. Now I am here. Maybe it's time to start dancing.

I had the feeling, as I gathered both groups (men and women) around me, that perhaps some of them have already left. Maybe they were freed by the mere fact of my finally gaining some insight into the situation.

Throughout my entire life I've been on very familiar terms with melancholia. Perhaps the bitter/sweet knowledge of what could very well be my life's work, consisting of freeing the spirits "trapped" here on this spot of ground, has been a part of my very nature since the beginning, but I just didn't understand it. Maybe those who still linger here at the Shaman Circle and Medicine Wheel had a love for this place that was so great they "thought" it into the astral plane and stayed on. Maybe it became their Consensus Reality.

We'll see. The future will bring more insight, I'm sure.

Perhaps all this forms the basis for the final journal entry I'll share with you in this chapter. Notice that the following dream occurred three months *before* the OBE entry just quoted. Did one influence the other? Are they connected? I'll just let the words I wrote at the time speak for themselves:

September 8, 2017
"Dance, shaman, dance. Dance and change the world!"

In my dream I was dancing at the Shaman Circle. I was accompanied by many others. There was no room for ego. There was no need for it. We were many. Each one of us was separate, but part of an eternal dance. There was no "I." Only "We." We were not moving. The world was moving beneath us. We were creating the world and molding it.

I always felt my purpose was to change the world.

That's why Grouse is my totem. That's why dance was so sacred to me that I couldn't profane it by using it as mere entertainment.

"Dance, shaman, dance. Dance and change the world!"

Some Final Thoughts

As I read and re-read these entries from my journal I'm struck, over and over, by a quality pervading them that I can only call self-aggrandizement. What kind of colossal ego does it take to think you are so important? Who really believes their task is to change the world? Really?

The only thing I can fall back on in response to such self-criticism is my strong and growing belief that every one of us comes into this world with a task to fulfill. It probably takes countless lifetimes to get it done, but everyone is a hero in that we all found the courage to submit to be born into this difficult, rough and tumble, world.

The Buddha had it right when he began his *Four Noble Truths* by declaring, "All life is suffering."

I've come to believe that it takes great courage to create a world and then enter into it, willingly and with full intention, knowing that to do so means leaving behind the memory of its purpose and taking on the subjective feeling that you are unique and alone in a great, seemingly endless, cosmos. But it's the only way to fully experience material life in this perception realm.

For two thousand years theologians have argued about whether or not a historical Jesus ever knew that he was a Son of God. One camp quotes scripture verses that seem to say he always knew exactly what his mission was, even when he was a young boy. The other selects different scriptures which indicate that Jesus only gradually came to discover that he was a Son of God.

Some scholars say that if he understood who he really was he couldn't have faced life as a true man—that the only way he could fulfill his appointed task was to have no knowledge available to him than isn't available to us. This, they declare, is the true significance of God becoming human. To do so fully, God must have no help beyond that given to each and every one of us. Otherwise the incarnation is a sham. This group teaches that he left all the powers and knowledge of heaven behind to become a man.

Others, however, believe that because Jesus was a member of the trinity he must always be, in some sense, God—that he must always be aware that he created the very society that was about to execute him. Only then could he truly forgive them.

It's a tough argument, either way. But let's take it out of its historical context and make it practical.

I have claimed that, in a very real way, *you* are the creator of your life—that you wrote the play in which you now star. I have further said that OBEs are a way of moving out from the stage and into the audience—that your five senses, aided by a subjective feeling of time, have deceived you. They have made you believe what I call the Great Illusion. I have attempted to rip the screen of the illusion down, exposing the manipulator behind the scenes. And that manipulator is you.

I don't think your eternal destiny somehow hangs in the balance. You are not on trial. You will not be judged on the basis of your choices. Maybe those choices are even predestined in the sense that before you were born you already decided, for whatever reason, whether or not you would see through the illusion in this life.

But to use that as an excuse *not* to try is to submit to fatalism.

Not everyone should intentionally engage an OBE during their lifetime. I'm not espousing some kind of religion. People who have OBEs are not "better" or "more spiritual" than anyone else. There is not, and should never be, some kind of exclusive OBE "club."

But if the opportunity is there, and you want to seek it out, why not?

For me the opportunity came late in life. In my case, that is no doubt as it should have been.

Some of you may remember "imaginary friends" from your childhood that gradually disappeared as society convinced you such things were impossible. In your case, OBEs may reunite you with long-lost soul mates.

Still others may have once received help from "outside" at a pertinent time. Perhaps you were sick and near death. Maybe you were mourning the loss of a loved one.

Some of you are just curious. A healthy curiosity is never a bad thing!

Whatever your reason, you now have a method. It's not the only way, but it will work for the vast majority of people who give it a sincere try.

Remember the basics: *30 minutes a day for at least 30 days.*

Let's review.

First, the overall plan:
- Make the Decision
- Stick To It
- Develop a System
- Focus, Focus, Focus!
- Stay Calm
- Keep a Journal

Next, meditate, concentrating on these attitudes:
- Stillness of heart
- Stillness of mind
- Stillness of body

Then, watch for help that is offered:

- Spirit guides come in an almost infinite variety of forms.
- The form you encounter will be a form you will recognize, based on your past experience. In other words, your brain will sort through your personal "rolodex" of experiences and choose to explain what is basically unexplainable by selecting a form you can most easily identify and feel comfortable with.
- Remember that your spirit guides probably don't really look the way they appear to you. It's only an approximation. But that's not important. It's about the message, not the messenger. Trust it!

To this I now offer the final piece of advice. You are a hero. Engaging an OBE involves a heroic journey to other realms. You have faced the trials of commitment, made the journey, and returned with your own holy grail. You are an ambassador to foreign worlds. You are contributing, even if only in a small way, to human evolution. Whatever happens to you during an OBE has a purpose, with cosmic consequences. I can't predict what that purpose will be, but in shamanic tradition it usually involves receiving some kind of help. It wouldn't come to you if you didn't need it and if you weren't either ready for it now or soon will be. The fruits of that journey are meant to be shared with others.

That being said, here's that final piece of advice:

- Be grateful!
- Share what you learn with others, either in word or in deed.
- Make the world a better place!

TEN
SUMMING IT ALL UP

The human mind is the laboratory of the new physics.
It already is tuned into the past and future, making existential
certainties out of probable realities. It does this simply by observing.
Observing oneself in a dream. Observing oneself in this world
when awake. Observing the action of observing.
Fred Alan Wolf in *Parallel Universes*

Choosing Your Future

In our familiar perception realm, things usually tend to make sense. A minute is always a minute (unless you're waiting for an elevator), a mile is always a mile (unless you're stuck in traffic), for every action there is an equal and opposite reaction (unless you're having an argument), and what goes around comes around (whatever that means).

But, as we have seen, out in the *Quantum Akashic Field*, strange things happen. An electron can appear and disappear, and then appear somewhere else, perhaps even in two places at the same time. Infinitesimal points don't show up until you look for them. Schrodinger's cat is alive and dead at the same time. Time can move in two directions, or it can stand still, or cease altogether. Energy can move faster than the speed of light, inflating to almost immeasurable distances in less than a tiny fraction of a second.

And if that weren't enough, there's the strange phenomenon called the *Observer Effect*. Things don't happen unless someone or something is watching.

So who was present to observe the Big Bang?

"It was a singularity," we are told. "It was a one-time event."

But according to a strict interpretation of quantum physics, such a thing cannot happen. There *had* to be an observer. That's one of the hard and fast rules.

Physicists get really nervous when you talk about such things. You can tell because the amount of bluster and feigned exasperation with "laypeople who don't understand math" usually rises precipitously.

But, as the old-time preachers used to say, "When your argument breaks down, pound the pulpit and shout like hell!" You see it in religion and politics all the time. You've probably experienced it at a Thanksgiving family dinner. You'll also find it in the sciences. It's very common.

There are some physicists, however, who take this argument seriously. "Who was the original observer?" they ask.

It's a good question that deserves a good answer. It also takes us to the heart of the Out-of-Body Experience.

We may need to get a bit technical for a minute, but stick with me.

One way of approaching the problem, without retreating into an easy, if un-provable, "God" hypothesis, is to remove time from the formula. It sounds like cheating, but according to the mathematics of the quantum world, it's a perfectly logical, if counter-intuitive, way of finding a solution.

Up here in our perception realm, our senses demand that we account for the passing of time. It seems to be hard-wired into the system. But down in the quantum world, time is an illusion. Past, present, and future all exist together, simultaneously. Perhaps even side by side, as separate dimensions. Thus, a choice made by an observer in what we call the future can trigger a collapse of energy into a predictable and material course of action in what we call the past.

How's that for an idea? The future can bring about the present, and the present can shape the past! In other words, what happens to you might well be the result of a choice that a future "you" made in order to bring about the very reality that future "you" is currently experiencing.

I know that sounds like a silly word game. But trust me. Serious scientists are really thinking about this. Oh, they use different terminology, such as holograms, space-time observer effects, and quantum leaps. That gives the whole concept a higher status in academia. Such ideas, however, are out there and real.

But to limit this kind of thinking to the hypothetical and surreal is to ignore its practical possibilities. Now we start to close in on OBEs.

Consider premonitions and déjà vu, for instance. Have you ever had the feeling that you knew something was going to happen before it happened? Have you done something and immediately felt you had done it before? Almost everyone has had such experiences, but no one knows how and why they occur.

Here's a possible explanation: What if you glimpsed, for a brief moment, the future as it exists in a parallel dimension?

Now let's make this even more practical.

Have you ever watched an athlete, let's say a pole vaulter, during a track and field event, pause and stare intently at the bar he is attempting to clear, before starting his approach? He is engaging in a common practice called *visualization*. He is picturing himself successfully completing his jump. He won't proceed until he has a clear picture of what he will accomplish.

You see this all the time these days. Golfers picture the shot they are about to take. Archers see only the small center of the target. Tennis players visualize their next serve. It's a common technique.

What these people are doing, probably without thinking about it in quantum terms, is selecting a specific future, eliminating all others, and then allowing that chosen course of action to proceed. When you watch athletes do this, you are looking at quantum reality in action. A decision is selected and observed as a completed event in the future. Then the appropriate motions proceed to produce the results in "real" time. You might even say that all the preparation and training leading up that point was predetermined by the actual event itself. Every moment of preparation was done with this goal in sight. So, in a sense, the future dictated the past.

In a way, you can call it meditation in action—deliberate, focused, one-point meditation. The participant eliminates all but the observed result, and then brings about that result in time.

Let's move away from the high-falutin' language and existential word-games for a moment and bring this concept down to earth. Once again, I retreat to that which I personally have experienced.

Example #1: Quantum Athletics

There have been a few times in my life when I experienced what is now called visualization—selecting a specific future that already seemed set in stone. The first time it happened to me was back in 1963. I was 17 years old on a beautiful fall day in early October.

I've always liked sports, and although I wasn't much of a competitive athlete, I've enjoyed running, long-distance biking, basketball, and soccer. I remember a particular day when I was playing soccer in gym class. I doubt if anyone else who participated in this particular game remembers it. It had no special meaning, per se. It was just a gym class soccer game. But it has been etched in my mind ever since it happened. I don't know what the final score was or even if we won or lost the game. I don't remember who was on my team, what they looked like, or what their names were. But I still see their forms on the field.

What I do remember is playing defense, intercepting a pass right in front of our goal, and glancing up the field. In a moment forever frozen in time, I knew exactly what was about to happen. I didn't decide what to do. I didn't form a plan. But in that instant I saw myself dribbling downfield to my left, going around two defenders as if they were standing still, being jostled by a third but staying on my feet while approaching the opposing goal, and then kicking a left-footed goal into the upper right hand corner of the net, just over the goalie's outstretched arms.

It happened just like that. Carrying out the vision was effortless. I was more a spectator than a participant. I can still see it unwinding in my mind like a video tape.

Since then I have heard top-echelon athletes talk about being "in the zone," and I think I understand exactly what they mean. It was as if I saw the future in a moment of time.

Now, remember that this was an unimportant event in an uneventful gym class during a typical high school day. At the time I knew nothing about quantum reality, déjà vu, visualizing, or parallel realities. I barely knew anything about soccer. So why did it stick with me, indelibly etched on my mind, for the last fifty-four years?

I'm convinced that, in that moment, something completely out of my ordinary perception happened. Totally by accident, without any intention at all, I "observed" and "chose" a particular future. Or, to put it another way, a completed future act, one of many that might have occurred, somehow reached back and compelled me to follow a pre-selected course of action.

The fact that it was "unimportant" doesn't matter. In fact, it makes it more compelling. Every act, every choice we make along this journey we call life, no matter how insignificant it seems at the time, could very well be leading toward what theologian/philosopher Pierre de Chardin once called an *Omega Point*. His idea was that we are not evolving *from* something in the past as much as we are evolving *toward* something in the future.

If he was right, that *something* is nothing less than a fully completed "you." Through countless lives, you are now in the process of becoming that which, in fact, you already are—a completed human being who already exists in what I have called the *Quantum Akashic Field*. In an OBE, when you separate from the information-tyranny of your five senses and the illusion of time, you actually experience this presence in the form of the Watcher, your "Higher Power," your spirit guide and constant companion, your Sobuko.

On that October day so long ago, the principles of quantum physics tell me that I probably experienced a number of different outcomes on that soccer field, all in separate parallel dimensions or alternate realities. In one such reality, I scored the goal I now remember. In another, I missed the shot. In yet another, I tripped and fell. Each "me" had the subjective feeling of living in the only reality. But the Watcher saw and experienced them all. This is called the *Many Worlds Theory* of quantum physics, in which every possible outcome of every observation is realized somewhere, somehow.

Thus it is with every course of action we experience in our lives. Every one, with all the objective and subjective feelings and emotions associated with it, is recorded in Akasha.

If this is true, then every choice depends on us. That's called *free will* and it's what we experience in any particular perception realm. But the end result includes every possibility. That's called *predestination* and exists in Akasha. Thus both are true. Both are real.

OBEs allow us to become conscious of those choices and, freed from the illusion produced by our senses, experience different perception realms.

Here's a practical application of this theory:

If you made bad choices in your past, choices you are ashamed of, choices you wish you could take back, choices you wish had different consequences, you can now put those behind you. They are part of a much greater arc of existence. You can forgive yourself and move on.

Example #2: Quantum Music

When I was a senior in high school I won an international music competition held at the National Music Camp in Interlochen, Michigan. I was a trombonist, and the prize was the opportunity to play a concerto with a symphony orchestra. I chose a piece written by Gordon Jacob. In the first movement there is a two-measure monster that gave me fits. Over the course of four short beats and three notes, it calls for the performer to play first a high D, and then a low pedal G. That's a span of more than three and a half octaves—not an inviting prospect. Mechanically it's very difficult. Musically it works. Doing it in public in front of 500 or more people can be terrifying to a high school kid.

No amount of practice can prepare you for such an occasion. You work and work, of course, but when you get on stage you remember the misses as well as the hits, and wonder which it will be on this particular night.

But something happened that, just like my soccer experience, stayed with me over the years. While walking out on the stage and hearing the applause after my introduction, I somehow decided I was going to be perfect. I was going to play the entire piece and not miss a note. I was going to find the meaning behind the music and be a vehicle, not just a producer, of the composer's intention. In other words, I was about to *channel* music, not *make* it. It was going to come from beyond—the home of the muse—*through* me and out to the audience.

And that's what happened. I found myself being more a spectator than a musician, a member of the audience rather than a performer on stage. When it came time to tackle the difficult passage in question, I knew before I played it that it would go as the composer intended. I played the whole piece as if I were in the middle of a meditation. There was no "me" and "them." There was no time or tempo. There was only music that demanded to be released, honored, and celebrated.

Since then I have played countless times in public. I earned a Bachelor's degree and began a career in music; teaching, conducting, and performing. I often experienced being a channel for the muse. It became a "normal" thing as I progressed. But that summer night, onstage at Interlochen, was the first time, and has stayed with me forever.

I have come to believe that these bodies of ours are *always* channels for energies bigger than we normally understand. Everything we do has cosmic consequences. Zen Buddhists teach us that even a lowly activity such as washing dishes can, and should, be an intentional meditation. According to them, planting a flower, knitting a sweater, typing a sentence, or brushing your teeth, can all be considered a prayer. Maybe this is what the Apostle Paul meant when he encouraged us to "pray without ceasing" (1st Thessalonians 5:17).

This doesn't mean we can be lazy in our preparation. That night long ago, when I played the way I did, would not have happened had I not spent humongous amounts of time in a practice room for years and years. It was there that the instrument and I had become one. My trombone was an expression of me just as I was an expression of music. Successful performances of real music are not accidental. They come only after a lot of effort.

It's exactly the same when it comes to OBEs. Sure, there are those who stumble into one and consider it a mystical experience. But:

The more you practice, the easier it will be to find a state of stillness and the grace of a calm interior. Moving outside your normal perception realm can happen by accident, but it happens more consistently with practice.

Example #3: Quantum Board-Breaking and Other Matters

Bruce Lee, the founder of *Jeet Kune Do*, one of the many Kung Fu styles of martial art, used to instruct his students that when they were throwing a punch they needed to aim at a point two inches past the target.

I tried to remember that when I first started breaking boards with my fists. (Why did I feel the need to learn how to do that? To this day, I haven't the faintest idea!)

When you learn to think "past the target," the board you are trying to break no longer occupies your mind. It is simply an obstacle in the way to your true goal. It almost ceases to exist. You focus on your target. Everything in between—air, the board, and external distractions—isn't even there. It's just you and an imaginary point two inches on the other side of the board. When you break through the board while achieving your objective, you never even feel it.

I think about that sometimes when I sit down to meditate. I concentrate on a point two inches in front of my forehead. If I do it right, everything else ceases to exist. There are no distractions. I go right past worrying about whether or not I remembered to do something I was supposed to do. I don't pay any attention to responsibilities that will claim my attention when I'm finished. Those thoughts are there, but they are mere distractions to be ignored. My five senses, and all their frantic input, become an obstacle that I pass right through on my way to the goal.

It sounds easier than it is. Sometimes I succeed. Usually I don't. It's a humbling experience.

But when it works, it can change your life:

January 10, 2018

It's been a while since I had an OBE and I'm getting a little discouraged. Life has pretty much nailed me down to the typical problems everyone faces nowadays. Most writers don't make any money to speak of, and even though Barb and I have trimmed our expenses to the bone, the economic powers-that-be seem to continually raise the price of the bone. I'm discouraged about the negativity that is so prevalent today. I used to enjoy following old friends on Facebook, but today's social media runs toward political diatribe and partisan rant. It's no fun. Besides that, I'm getting older and can't physically do what I used to do. Fatigue and soreness tend to bring you down spiritually and mentally. If all that wasn't enough, I've been struggling lately with typical writer/ego problems. As a writer I want my work to be successful. That means I need to attract an audience. But when you write about the kind of spirituality-type subjects I write about, there's a very fine line between success and ego. I'm reminded of the apocryphal church who once gave their pastor an award. It was a medal that proclaimed him to be a humble Christian. Then they took it away from him when he wore it with pride.

All this was going on at 3:00 this morning when it came time to meditate. I really didn't want to get up and move away from the warm bed, but somehow felt an obligation. That's not conducive to the peace and serenity needed to slow down enough to be at all successful. To make a long story short, I was expecting another failure. Meditation seemed a waste of time—time that could better be spent sleeping. But I was awake, so, mentally complaining all the way, I made my way to my chair, read for a few minutes, and then donned my headphones and turned on some music.

I've been working on a pet theory of mine that postulates there's more to inducing OBEs then simply bypassing the five senses. I've begun to suspect that time itself is part of the process. As long as we are caught in the so-called "stream" of time, we are imprisoned within this particular universe. Space and time are connected. They are dimensions of the same universe. When we feel locked into time, we feel locked into this particular cosmic landscape.

It was rough. My brain seemed to be even jumpier than normal. Thought after random thought filled my head. But somehow, I don't know how, I managed to arrive at a place of peace and serenity long enough to experience a moment of perfect stillness. That was all it took.

I felt myself falling backward, slipping down and seemingly into the earth. This hasn't happened to me often before, and it was so intriguing I was able to go with it, just out of curiosity. I've quite often experienced moving up and out, but this time it was definitely down. My thought was that I was experiencing a shamanic journey down to the first, lower world, rather than the third, upper world. In traditional shamanic thought, there are three worlds. The lower is the world of animal spirits and creatures of the earth. The middle is the world we inhabit during our waking lives. The upper is the light and airy place of fairies, angels, and flying creatures. During OBEs I've often experienced the middle and upper worlds. This was different and I was immediately fascinated.

Following my own rules of remaining calm and observant, I found myself in a place of jungle and rocks. It was dense and close. Out of the tangled growth I could see very clearly the head and front portion of a large serpent, a snake who waved its head back and forth toward me, weaving an almost hypnotic spell. It was not at all frightening. Just the opposite, in fact. I was intrigued and fascinated.

Suddenly I found myself in the presence of an entity who seemed quite at home. He was a friendly sort, leprechaun-ish in appearance, with a short, wiry beard and typical round, old face. He asked me, without speaking, of course, but by something that can only be described as some sort of telepathy, if I was interested in exploring a bit.

I responded in the affirmative, of course. This was good stuff!

For some reason I started to share my worries with him. He seemed a good sort, and I felt he might be able to help. I laid the whole writer/book-selling/ego/intentional thing on him and asked if he could assist me. Maybe he could help sell some books. That kind of thing. He was quite positive about the whole situation. Of course he could help. That's what spirit guides did!

But immediately something changed. I looked up and across a great chasm that had suddenly appeared and saw a large bear staring at me. (The bear, I need to add, is one of Barb's most powerful totem animals.) The bear didn't move. It just stood there, staring intently. There was no question but that the bear was sending me a message.

Immediately a poem came fully to mind and seemed to hang in the air before me. During my experience I could remember every word of that poem. Later, when I finished my trip and returned back to my senses, I couldn't remember all of it and had to look it up. But here is a relevant portion, thanks to a quick Internet search:

> "Once to every man and nation,
> Comes the moment to decide,
> In the strife of truth with falsehood,
> For the good or evil side...
> Though the cause of evil prosper,
> Yet the truth alone is strong;
> Though her portion be the scaffold,
> And upon the throne be wrong;
> Yet that scaffold sways the future,
> And behind the dim unknown,
> Standeth God within the shadow,
> Keeping watch above His own."
>
> **James Russell Lowell**

I can't explain what happened next. I understood it within a Christian context, but I don't believe it is necessarily linked to Christianity alone. It's just that Christianity, being my background tradition, is more familiar to me than other religions. Undoubtedly, the form was later interpreted by my waking brain within that context.

I became aware that I had a choice to make. The leprechaun-ish entity would probably help me if I asked, but I would lose something in the bargain. Bible texts seemed highlighted before my eyes.

"Seek ye first the kingdom of God … and all the rest will be added unto you."
Matthew 6:33

"What does it profit someone if they gain the whole world but lose their soul?"
Matthew 16:26

I was aware of a very great temptation being offered me. I could become a successful writer and influence many people. But if that was the reason for my writing, to gain personal fame and fortune, I would lose something valuable. Perhaps even my very soul.

The other-worldly entity seemed to know exactly what I was thinking.

"But aren't you willing to offer your soul as payment if it will help countless others? Isn't that the Christian message? Isn't that what Jesus did?"

At this point I have to explain something. I consider myself a Christian, but I'm not sure if a historical Jesus ever existed. I don't really believe in most interpretations of a historical crucifixion. To me, it doesn't matter if such a thing ever took place as the Bible represents it. That doesn't make the message of it any less real. The important thing, according to my belief system, is the message, not the event itself.

But that didn't even really enter my head during this experience.

"Did Jesus really lose his soul?" I answered. "I think not! He did it out of love, not a desire for fame."

And in that moment, my whole life seemed to hang in the balance. I had a choice to make. Before me stood the friendly, leprechaun-like figure who was offering me my earthly dream. Across the great chasm stood a large bear who offered nothing, but seemed to stare into my very soul.

"Once to every man and nation comes the moment to decide…"

I chose the bear, and immediately returned to my body, dripping in sweat and trembling all over. There would be no more sleep that night. But I would remain, simply, Jim. I would write about what was in my heart and what I felt was important, even if no one else ever read my words.

. . .

I've thought about what happened for a few hours, now, and have come to some tentative conclusions.

I wonder if my previous OBEs were preparing me, somehow, for this choice. I've written before about my belief that I am, in some sense, the creator of my universe. As are we all. I've speculated that we enter into our own creations in order to experience life in a material context.

What if Hell really exists, and we are, to a certain extent, already in it? If Hell is defined as separation from God, then life consisting of an individual existence in a material world, cut off by our senses from God, our environment, and each other, certainly qualifies as separation. And like actors who play a role, if we lose ourselves in the part, if we forget who we really are, we might be destined to live life after life after life until we get it right and choose to remember what's important. It's called karma, and sometimes it's a real bitch.

When that happens to some people, they get so involved in the pursuit of success, riches and power, fame and fortune, that they get lost. We all know of people like that: Hitler, Stalin, some familiar political figures from American history, movie stars, musicians and other public figures. When they lose sight of who they are, they get lost. They are cut off from God. They wander in the wilderness, and it's a long way home. In another universe they might have chosen differently. But here, in this one, they failed. Sometimes they even caused untold hardship and death.

That's why this kind of book is so important. It also leads us to our final point:

There is a lot more significance in the cosmos than our earthly existence normally dreams of. If we don't wake up to that soon, we might be in real trouble.

Though the cause of evil prosper,
Yet the truth alone is strong;
Though her portion be the scaffold,
And upon the throne be wrong;
Yet that scaffold sways the future...

Final Thoughts

We've come a long way together. If you haven't yet tried, you are probably wondering if you can engage a successful OBE. Perhaps you've tentatively experimented a little. Maybe you've had some success. I hope so.

All I can promise is that there is more to this life than we ever dreamed of. Reality is far greater than our conception of it. You are one of millions trying to make sense out of what often seems to be chaotic and troublesome times. You are reaching out with open minds, hands, and hearts towards the glorious impossible. That's where we are all headed, eventually. You now have a front row seat.

As you part the curtain separating you from all other dimensions, worlds, parallel realities and alternate perception realms, know that there are spirit guides on distant shores, just as real as you are, who are calling out to you. They are evolving in their perception realms as you are evolving in yours. Know as well that just as voices behind you begin to fade into the distance, there are other voices on a distant shore, ready and willing to welcome a friendly visitor. All are part of a magnificent evolutionary procession.

Fear not, my friends. We are now, and always have been, in good hands.

Behind the dim unknown,
Standeth God within the shadow,
Keeping watch above His own.

Happy journeys!

FURTHER READING

Ashton, John and Tom Whyte. *The Quest for Paradise: Visions of Heaven and Eternity in the World's Myths and Religions*. New York, NY: Harper Collins, 2001.

Atwater, F. Holmes. *Captain of My Ship, Master of My Soul*. Charlottesville, VA: Hampton Roads Publishing, Inc., 2001.

Atwater, PMH. *We Live Forever: The Real Truth About Death*. Virginia Beach, VA. ARE Press, 2004.

Bolen, Jean Shinoda, MD. *Gods in Every Man*. San Francisco, CA: Harper and Row, 1989.

Broadhurst, Paul and Hamish Miller. *The Sun and the Serpent*. Cornwall, England: Pendragon Press, 2013.

Buhlman, William. *Adventures Beyond the Body*. New York, NY: Harper Collins, 1996.

———. *Adventures in the Afterlife*. Millsboro, Delaware: Osprey Press, 2013.

———. *The Secret of the Soul*. New York, NY: Harper Collins, 2001.

Campbell, Joseph with Bill Moyers. *The Power of Myth*. New York, NY: Bantam, Doubleday Dell Publishing Group, 1988.

Campbell, Joseph. *Transformations of Myth through Time*. New York, NY: Harper and Row, 1990.

Chopra, Depak and Leonard Mlodinonow. *War of the World View: Science Versus Spirituality*. New York, NY: Harmony Books, 2011.

Clark, Jerome. *Unexplained! Strange Sightings, Incredible Occurrences, and Puzzling Physical Phenomena* (Third Edition). Canton, MI: Visible Ink Press: 2013.

Cotterell, Arthur and Rachel Storm. *The Ultimate Encyclopedia of Mythology*. China: Hermes House, 1999.

DeLaney, Gayle, PH.D. *All About Dreams*. SanFrancisco, CA: Harper Collins, 1993.

Dennett, Daniel. *Darwin's Dangerous Idea: Evolution and the Meanings of Life*. New York, NY: Touchstone, 1996.

De Ropp, Robert S. *The Master Game: Pathways to Higher Consciousness*. New York, NY: Dell, 1989.

Ellwood, Robert S. and Barbara A. McGraw. *Many Peoples, Many Faiths: Women and Men in the World Religions*, 7th Edition. Upper Saddle River, NJ: Prentiss Hall, 2002.

Estes, Clarissa Pinkola. *Women Who Run With the Wolves: Myths and Stories of the Wild Woman Archetype*. New York, NY: Ballantine Books, 1992.

Fisher, Mary Pat and Lee W. Bailey. *An Anthology of Living Religions*. Upper Saddle River, NJ: Prentiss Hall, 2000.

Gaskell, G. A. *Dictionary of all Scriptures and Myths*. New York, NY: Gramercy Books, 1981.

Gould, Stephen J. *Rocks of Ages: Science and Religion in the Fullness of Life*. New York, NY: Ballantine Publishing Group, 1999.

Hancock, Graham. *Fingerprints of the Gods*. New York, NY: Three Rivers Press, 1995.

——. *Magicians of the Gods*. New York, NY: St. Martin's Press, 2015.

——. *Supernatural*. New York, NY: Disinformation Company Ltd., 2007.

——. *Underworld: The Mysterious Origins of Civilization*. New York, NY: Crown Publishers, Inc., 2002.

Harari, Yuval Noah. *Homo Deus: A Brief History of Tomorrow*. London: Penguin Random House, 2015.

——. *Sapiens: A Brief History of Humankind*. New York, NY: Harper Collins, 2015.

Harner, Michael. *Cave and Cosmos*. Berkeley, CA: North Atlantic Books, 2013.

——. *The Way of the Shaman*. San Francisco, CA: Harper & Row, 1980.

Harper, Tom. *The Pagan Christ*. Toronto, Canada: Thomas Allen Publishers, 2004.

Hick, John. *Classical and Contemporary Readings in the Philosophy of Religion*. Edgewood Cliffs, NJ: Prentiss Hall, Inc., 1964.

Highwater, Jamake. *The Primal Mind: Vision and Reality in Indian America*. New York, NY: Harper & Row Publishers, Inc., 1981.

Hitching, Francis. *Earth Magic*. New York, NY: William Morrow and Company, Inc., 1977.

Houston, Jean. *The Hero and the Goddess*. New York, NY: Ballantine Books, 1992.

Ingerman, Sandra and Hank Wesselman. *Awakening to the Spirit World: The Shamanic Path of Direct Revelation*. Boulder, CO: Sounds True, Inc., 2011.

Kapra, Fritjof. *The Tao of Physics: An Exploration of the Parallels Between Modern Physics and Eastern Mysticism*. Boston, MA: Shambala Publications, 1975.

Kauffman, Stuart A. *Reinventing the Sacred: A New View of Science, Reason, and Religion*. Philadelphia, PA: Basic Books, 2008.

Keck, L. Robert. *Sacred Eyes*. Indianapolis, IN: Knowledge Systems, Inc., 1992.

Keen, Jeffrey. *Consciousness, Intent, and the Structure of the Universe*. Victoria, BC: Trafford Publishing, 2005.

Lanza, Robert, MD with Bob Berman. *Biocentrism: How Life and Consciousness are the Keys to Understanding the True Nature of the Universe*. Dallas, TX: BenBella Books, Inc., 2009.

——— . *Beyond Biocentrism: Rethinking Time, Space, Consciousness, and the Illusion of Death.* Dallas, TX: BenBella Books, Inc., 2016.

Lao Tzu. Lau D. C. Translator. *Tao Te Ching.* New York, NY: Penguin Books, 1963.

Laszlo, Ervin. *Science and the Akashic Field: An Integral Theory of Everything, Updated Second Edition.* Rochester, VT: Inner Traditions, 2007.

——— . *The Akashic Experience: Science and the Cosmic Memory Field.* Rochester, VT: Inner Traditions, 2009.

——— . *The Whispering Pond: A Personal Guide to the Emerging Vision of Science.* Rockport, MA: Element Books, Inc., 1996.

Macrone, Michael. *By Jove!: Brush Up Your Mythology.* New York, NY: Harper Collins, 1992.

Mails, Thomas E. *Dancing in the Paths of the Ancestors.* New York, NY: Marlowe & Co., 1999.

Mavor, James W. and Byron E. Dix. *Manitou.* Rochester, VT: Inner Traditions International, 1989.

Monroe, Robert A. *Far Journeys.* New York, NY: Doubleday, 1985.

——— . *Journeys Out of the Body.* New York, NY: Doubleday, 1971.

——— . *Ultimate Journey.* New York, NY: Doubleday, 1994.

Morris, Desmond. *The Naked Ape.* New York, NY: Dell Publishing Co., Inc., 1973.

Peterson, Robert. *Out of Body Experiences.* Charlottesville, VA: Hampton Roads Publishing Co., Inc., 1997.

Radin, Dean. *Entangled Minds.* New York, NY: Simon and Schuster, 2006.

——— . *Real Magic: Ancient Wisdom, Modern Science, and a Guide to the Secret Power of the Universe.* New York, NY: Harmony Books, 2018.

——— . *Supernormal: Science, Yoga and the Evidence for Extraordinary Abilities.* New York, NY: Random House, Inc., 2013.

——— . *The Conscious Universe: The Scientific Truth of Psychic Phenomena.* San Francisco, CA: Harper Collins, 1997.

Ross, T. Edward and Richard D. Wright. *The Divining Mind: A Guide to Dowsing and Self Awareness.* Rochester, VT: Destiny Books, 1990.

Selbie, Joseph. *The Physics of God.* Wayne, NJ: The Career Press, Inc., 2018.

Stevenson, Ian, M.D. *Children Who Remember Past Lives: A Question of Reincarnation.* Jefferson, NC: McFarland & Company, 2021.

Strassman, Rick. *DMT: The Spirit Molecule.* Rochester, VT: Park Street Press, 2001.

——— . *DMT and the Soul of Prophecy.* Rochester, VT: Park Street Press, 2014.

——— . *Inner Paths to Outer Space: Journeys to Alien Worlds through Psychedelics and other Spiritual Technologies.* Rochester, VT: Park Street Press, 2008.

Taylor, Albert. *Soul Traveler: A Guide to Out of Body Experiences and the Wonders Beyond*. Covena, CA: Verity Press Publishing, 1996.

Tucker, Jim B. M.D. *Life Before Life: Children's Memories of Previous Lives*. New York, NY: St. Martin's Press, 2005.

Weiss, Brian L. M.D. *Many Lives, Many Masters*. New York, NY: Simon and Schuster, Inc., 1988.

——. *Same Soul, Many Masters*. New York, NY: Simon and Schuster, Inc., 2004.

——. *Where Reincarnation and Biology Intersect*. Westport, CT: Greenwood Publishing Group, 1997.

Willis, Jim. *Ancient Gods: Lost Histories, Hidden Truths and the Conspiracy of Silence*. Detroit, MI: Visible Ink Press, 2016.

——. *The Dragon Awakes: Rediscovering Earth Energy in the Age of Science*. Daytona Beach, FL: Dragon Publishing Co., 2014.

——. *The Religion Book: Places, Prophets, Saints and Seers*. Detroit, MI: Visible Ink Press, 2004.

——. *Supernatural Gods: Spiritual Mysteries, Psychic Experiences and Scientific Truths*. Detroit, MI: Visible Ink Press, 2017.

Wolf, Fred Alan. *Parallel Universes: The Search for Other Worlds*. New York, NY: Simon and Schuster, 1988.

Wright, Patricia C. and Richard D. Wright. *The Divining Heart*. Rochester, VT: Destiny Books, 1994.

ACKNOWLEDGMENTS

An entry from my dream journal and an account of my visit to the English town of Fenny Compton which are used in this book were briefly quoted in *Supernatural Gods: Spiritual Mysteries, Psychic Experiences and Scientific Truths,* published by Visible Ink Press in 2017. I rewrote them to fit this current context and acknowledged their previous use within the text, but I want to reiterate that they are here used by permission. Thanks to Roger Janecke and the good folks at VIP!

Barbara Willis, my wife of 16 years and my partner during the course of thousands more over the course of many lives, reads, comments on, and edits everything I write. She was the one who coined the term "perception realm." When we moved to this special place in South Carolina, little did we know that she was coming home. Rock on, Barb!

Jan Willis, my daughter, tech support, PR consultant and Faery aficionado par excellence, serves as my editor and commentator alongside Barb. The only downside to the trio is that I can sometimes be out-voted. To make things worse, they're usually right. Thanks, Jan!

Annie Wilder, my literary agent, has proved to be an invaluable resource when it comes to shepherding a book from an idea to a published product. Annie, you're a jewel!

Our generation is blessed with some great thinkers and doers. Ervin Lazlo, Deepak Chopra, Dean Radin, William Buhlman, Fred Alan Wolf, Michael Harner, Hank Wessleman, Sandra Ingerman, and many more whose work is listed in the Bibliography have all contributed, and continue to contribute, to our understanding of what's really going on in the wild and wonderful cosmos we inhabit. May their kind continue to lead us into a hopeful future.

Gerry Bailey became a long-distance friend after he wrote to tell me that he appreciated my book, *Ancient Gods*. Since then he has shared some of his life story with me. I soon found him to be a kindred soul, but one who was born with natural OBE talents that I've needed to work to develop. Because he grew up in the generation that preceded mine, our culture forced him to make difficult choices that steered him away from his natural abilities. But his encouragement has been invaluable. He read both *Supernatural Gods* and this book before the editors even had a chance to work on them. Thanks Gerry. You've become a treasured friend!

ABOUT THE AUTHOR

Jim Willis is the author of eleven books on religion and spirituality in the 21st century, along with many magazine articles on topics ranging from earth energies to ancient civilizations. He was an ordained minister for more than forty years while also working part-time as a carpenter, musician, the host of his own drive-time radio show, an arts council director, and adjunct college professor in the fields of World Religions and Instrumental Music.

For more information on Jim Willis visit his website:
www.jimwillis.net

Quantum World 88→